The Iliad

Interpreted for Real Estate Investors

The Hidden Human Conflicts Behind Successful Real Estate Deals

---

ANCIENT WISDOM HACKS

Publisher: NX Inc

Third Edition

Table of Contents

Introduction – Why Homer Still Pays Rent

When you strip away the spears, gods, and bronze, *The Iliad* is a 2,700-year-old playbook on how groups marshal resources, handle risk, and fight for high-value assets under brutal uncertainty. Real-estate markets aren't battlefields, but capital is finite, competitors are ruthless, and every acquisition is a siege on today's price for tomorrow's payoff. Homer's heroes model the same disciplines top investors need: assembling a loyal team, defining the one prize worth the grind, protecting supply lines, and exiting before hubris torches the win. Flip the helmets for hard hats and the poem becomes field intel for anyone who writes earnest-money checks instead of epic verse.

This book turns sixteen pivotal moments from the Trojan War into straight-up strategy you can apply at the next property walkthrough. **Part I, "Gearing Up for War,"** covers market recon, emotional discipline, and locking your investment thesis. **Part II, "Inside the Campaign,"** dives into creative financing, asset management, and surviving liquidity crunches when the gods—read: Fed, city council, or bond market—change the rules overnight. **Part III, "Exit, Tribute, and Legacy,"** drills into negotiation, timing your sale or refinance, and building a portfolio that outlives you. Each chapter ends with "Field Orders": concise action steps, worksheets, and scorecards so the lessons don't stay myth—they move cash.

Read this intro, gear up, and march in. The Trojans never saw the horse coming; your competition won't see Homer on your balance sheet.

Chapter 1 — The Gathering of Kings (Market Recon)

The Lesson in Homeric Context: Agamemnon Unites Fractious Allies

Bronze tangles with bronze, banners snap in the sea wind, and the plain before Troy glitters with a thousand campfires. The coalition massed under Agamemnon is no tight-knit regiment but a nervous merger of nearly fifty warlords, each with private grudges, local dialects, rival gods, and separate payrolls. Homer spends an entire book—the famous Catalogue of Ships—to remind us how disparate the Greek armada really is. Even before the first spear is thrown, Agamemnon must persuade, threaten, flatter, and coordinate a management team whose only shared asset is grievance.

> "He stood among them, lord of men, and cried,
> 'Friends, Danaan warriors, comrades of my youth,
> disaster swells unless our hearts unite.'"

In that blunt speech (Butler's translation), two truths leak out. First, no single hero, not even the high king, can sack a fortified city alone. Second, the enemy inside the tent—ego, distrust, siloed information—can rout an army faster than any Trojan sortie. Agamemnon's gift is less about swordplay and more about orchestrating clashing assets into a focused strike. He inventories talents (Ajax's brute strength, Odysseus's brains, Achilles' shock force), matches resources to tactics, and binds them with a clear if brutal incentive scheme: fame, plunder, and a swift sail home.

Even when the coalition wobbles—Achilles' withdrawal, internecine brawls, the near-mutiny stirred by Thersites—Agamemnon works the room. He calls councils at dawn, hosts sacrificial feasts that double as board meetings, and sometimes swallows his own pride to keep the campaign solvent. His success, partial and costly though it is, proves a single principle: a fractured band of competent specialists, if well-aligned, can outperform any lone star.

Real-estate investors rarely swing spears, yet they, too, pursue fortified targets—properties defended by price resistance, bidding wars, or local politics. The modern investor who believes she can marshal equity, debt, entitlements, inspections, rehab crews, and leasing without a coalition is replaying Achilles sulking in his tent: proud, potent, and stalled.

Translating Homer to Modern Deal-Making: Building Your Power Team

Recon Is Social Before It's Spatial

Market reconnaissance sounds like spreadsheets and census tracts, but the first terrain you must map is human. Brokers with pocket listings, lenders who whisper rate moves, attorneys who smell zoning shifts—these players clear the fog of war long before CoStar does. Without them you are recon blind, stuck at the beachhead like raw recruits deciphering smoke signals.

Think of Agamemnon's first council as the original due-diligence huddle. He doesn't raid Troy on day one; he canvasses allies, asks what each city-state can field, gauges supply lines, and confirms the shared objective. In real-estate terms, that means meeting every professional who might touch your deal well before a live target appears. You map capacity, cost, temperament, and motivation. You look for hidden frictions: a broker whose cousin sits on the planning board (gold) or a contractor in private litigation (landmine).

> "He called to the chiefs by name, from the swift ships they came in rows,
>   each man eager to know his place in the assault."

That line rings today whenever a sponsor emails a deal deck, cc's the title agent, blind-cc's the mezz lender, and schedules a Zoom for eight a.m. Everyone wants to know the task list, the payout, and who drives. Hierarchy clarifies urgency; ambiguity breeds Achilles-grade anger.

Role Parallels: From Myrmidons to Mortgage Bankers

- **Agamemnon → Lead Sponsor / Managing Member**
  He shoulders vision risk: picks the battlefield, sets timeline, raises capital.

- **Nestor → Senior Adviser / Attorney**
  The old warrior with "words sweet as honey yet sharp as steel" mirrors the seasoned lawyer who has seen every auction, lien, and tenant uprising.

- **Odysseus → Broker / Acquisition Specialist**
  Fluent across cultures, slippery with words, Odysseus scouts deals others can't access, spins objections into accord, and finds passages through bureaucratic choke points.

- **Achilles → Specialist Contractor or Value-Add Crew Chief**
  A storm weapon deployed at decisive moments—foundation lift, structural steel, adaptive reuse—expensive, temperamental, indispensable.

- **Diomedes → Lender Relationship Manager**
  Fearless when money needs to charge the line. Diomedes cuts through red tape, presses credit committees, and keeps loans moving while others hedge.

- **Ajax → Property Manager / Operations Lead**
  A wall of brute reliability. He holds the ships while heroes chase glory; a property manager holds occupancy above break-even while investors chase new acquisitions.

The analogy clarifies two secrets: (1) every role can sway outcome, and (2) no role can substitute for another without cost. Hire an aggressive broker but a lax attorney and you risk a title ambush. Postpone contractor bids and your pro-forma melts in the sun like wax.

Aligning Incentives—War Booty vs. Fee Stack

Greek kings fought for tangible spoil: cattle, tripods, carved chalices, women wrongly classified as "prizes." Today's coalition fights for less tangible but equally compelling spoils: acquisition fees, carried interest, points on the loan, workout bonuses. Misalign those and mutiny looms.

Agamemnon provokes Achilles by confiscating Briseis, not because he wants her but because he worries allies will see leniency as weakness. Likewise, an investor who renegotiates a contractor midway to shave costs may gain a short-term saving yet lose long-term loyalty. Better to widen the pot—offer performance bonuses for faster turnover or net-operating-income targets—than to snatch someone's "Briseis" after the march begins.

> "Not for the girl's sake only do I grieve," Achilles
> flares, "but because in all things you rage to sack
> what is another man's."

That line, shouted across the council, should be printed at the top of every joint-venture agreement: touch another man's profit share and you've lit a fuse no insurance covers.

Communication Cadence: Dawn Councils & Field Reports

In the poem, councils convene at sunrise, before rumors twist the day. The investor equivalent is the Monday-morning pipeline call. A broker drops intel on fresh listings; the lender flags DSCR ratios;

the attorney notes a change in municipal code. Speed stifles gossip and wrong assumptions.

Modern tools rarely equal the drama of Agamemnon lifting a sceptre among fifty kingdoms, yet Slack channels, shared data rooms, and weekly dashboards reenact the principle: speak early, update often, settle disputes in the open. Every delayed disclosure corrodes coalition morale.

Action Steps — Team-Mapping and Vetting

You now know why the gathering matters. Here's how to march the idea from myth into your notebook and then your balance sheet. Use these steps sequentially; shortcut one and you relive the night Ajax almost torches the ships while Achilles sulks.

1. Sketch the Campaign Tree

On a blank sheet, draw the target property at the center. Branch outward with every discipline that will touch it from first comp to final disposition. Expect at least these limbs:

- Acquisition Sourcing

- Capital Stack (Debt, Equity, Grants)

- Legal & Compliance

- Physical Due Diligence

- Construction / Value-Add

- Asset Management

- Disposition / Refi

Under each limb, leave five lines to list candidate allies.

2. Generate the Long List

Commit one hour to brute research. Comb your inbox, LinkedIn, local REI groups, chamber of commerce rosters. Dump every plausible broker, lender, attorney, contractor, inspector, architect, and manager onto the page—don't filter yet. This is Homer's Catalogue moment: quantity precedes quality.

3. Apply the Three-P Filter: Proof, Proximity, Philosophy

- **Proof**: Do they show war scars? You want HUD-1s, case studies, referrals, not résumés thick with fluff.

- **Proximity**: Do they operate where the property sits? Odysseus might speak multiple tongues, but he still needs footprints on Trojan soil.

- **Philosophy**: Do they take risk the way you do? A bank that hates bridge loans will stall your heavy-value-add deal.

Cross-out any candidate failing two of the three. Circle those who pass all three—they form your preliminary phalanx.

4. Conduct the Six-Call Gauntlet

You will next schedule six ten-minute calls. Each call focuses on one angle:

1. **Track Record Narrative** — "Tell me your proudest rescue of a busted deal."

2. **Communication Rhythm** — "How often will I hear from you unprompted?"

3. **Fee Transparency** — "Show me your last three invoices or term sheets."

4. **Network Depth** — "Name the three professionals you rely on most. May I call them?"

5. **Conflict Case Study** — "Describe a partnership that went sour and why."

6. **Growth Vision** — "Where will your firm be in five years and how does that help my deals?"

Keep a single sheet for each candidate. Mark one to five stars after every call on clarity, cultural fit, and willingness to put skin in the game.

5. Run the Trojan Wall Test

Before Agamemnon drags men to Troy, he tests morale by faking a retreat. Steal that tactic. Offer each shortlisted ally a micro-assignment that pays symbolic coin: a zoning lookup, a quick rent-comp chase, a sample underwriting. Watch who delivers on time, who ghosts, who over-delivers, and who nickel-and-dimes. Performance under trivial stakes predicts behavior when millions ride.

6. Draft the Coalition Charter

Write a one-page charter that states:

- Target property profile and thesis

- Roles and deliverables per ally

- High-level incentive structure (fees, shares, bonuses)

- Primary communication cadence

- Dispute-resolution method

Circulate it. Demand acknowledgments in writing. This document is your modern "oath of the Achaeans."

> "So swore they all, and their high king sealed the pact with wine and prayer."

You may skip the ox-blood sacrifice, but not the signed charter.

7. Implement the Vetting Checklist

Tick each box before awarding final mandates:

- Confirm license status with state boards

- Pull litigation history for the past five years

- Verify insurance and bonding levels

- Call at least two not-provided references

- Inspect sample work product (closing binder, draw schedule, lease audit)

- Stress-test availability (unexpected weekend call or tight deadline)

- Align termination clauses—no hostage fees if you end the contract

- Secure data-sharing agreements if sensitive financials pass through their hands

Only when all boxes read "clear" do you issue the green light.

8. Stage the Dawn Council

Hold an in-person or video kickoff. Agenda:

1. Re-state mission, timeline, and success metrics.

2. Review the action funnel from offer to close and onward to stabilization.

3. Assign single owners for each funnel stage—no fuzzy overlaps.

4. Establish a war room: shared folder tree, chat channels, naming conventions.

5. Schedule weekly cadence through first quarter post-close.

Close the meeting with one sentence each ally must finish: "If I see X risk forming, I will Y." Their answers pre-set escalation paths.

9. Monitor, Adjust, Celebrate

Agamemnon posts sentries at night and rewards valor at dawn. Translate that into monthly KPIs and public praise. Spotlight the contractor who hits a milestone early, the leasing agent who closes ten renewals in one week. Bonuses tied to shared upside turn competitors into guardians of the common pot.

10. Cull Without Hesitation

When Achilles refused to fight, the Greeks limped until crisis forced apology. Learn the lesson and cut underperformers early. Terminate the lender who drags commitment letters, the broker who hoards comps, the attorney who bills in koans. Your coalition is a living organism; excise infection before it reaches the heart.

- Map every skill node and list three candidates per node by tomorrow 1700 hours.

- Execute the six-call gauntlet on priority prospects within seven calendar days.

- Draft and circulate a coalition charter before issuing any letter of intent.

- Require tangible micro-deliverables from each ally inside two weeks. Fake retreat optional but recommended.

- Schedule the Dawn Council no later than forty-eight hours after mutual acceptance on a live deal.

Closing the Chapter

Homer shows us that empires crumble or rise on the chemistry of their coalitions. Agamemnon bullies, wheedles, and at times repents, but he never ignores the glue that holds disparate talents in formation. If you carry one image from this chapter into the street, let it be that night on the shore when Greek kings huddled by torchlight, voices drifting over the surf, each man agreeing that no single sword could breach Troy. Your real-estate conquests will demand the same confession of limitation—and the same discipline of alliance. Gather your kings now, while the ships are still on the sand. When the walls of your target property loom, it will be too late to draft the charter.

Chapter 2 — Achilles' Rage (Emotional Discipline)

The Flashpoint: Insult, Injury, and the Cost of Fury

"Sing, O goddess, the anger of Achilles son of Peleus, that brought countless ills upon the Achaeans." Homer fires that opening line like an arrow. Before we learn the names of cities or even the spark that lit the war, we meet rage—pure, incandescent, unfiltered. The poet wants us to know that one man's emotional storm can grind an entire army to dust.

Achilles is not slighted on the battlefield; he is slighted in the boardroom. Agamemnon confiscates Briseis, a prize of honor, and the world's best fighter folds his arms and parks his warship in the sand. In the smoky council tent he roars:

> "Greedy dog, shameless—can any Achaean obey you?
> I carried off no plunder equal to yours,
> yet you still take what is mine, aching to add one more prize
> to your hoard."

The quarrel is over ownership and reputation, not mortal danger. But ego transposes the grievance into an existential affront, and Achilles stalks away. The fallout is immediate: Greek casualties spike, morale craters, supply lines buckle. At one point, Hector's offensive surges so deep that the flames of burning ships shine on distant headlands. All because a champion let his pulse set the plan.

Rage is dramatic, yet subtler emotions—envy, panic, pride—can sabotage just as thoroughly. Homer dramatizes the largest version so no leader can miss the warning. The real tragedy is how familiar the scene still feels inside a modern deal room: an investor hard-passes on a lucrative property because a broker mispronounced his name; a lender retracts a term sheet after a junior partner needles his authority; a contractor walks off-site mid-rehab because change orders bruise her professional standing.

Modern Terrain: Where Emotions Hijack the Underwrite

Real-estate underwriting is sold as math: gross potential rent, expense ratio, internal rate of return. Whispered at conferences, though, is the truth that feelings dominate the delta between modeled success and market reality. Here are the ambush points:

- **Ego Inflation**
  The operator who boasts five-for-five flips in a rising market "knows" his next projection will hit sixteen percent IRR because he is, well, him. He rounds rents up, vacancies down, CapEx into the future. Eventually he buys the wrong asset at the wrong yield because the

spreadsheet served pride, not probability.

- **Fear Paralysis**
  Another investor pins monthly newsletters to the corkboard warning of recessions, elections, pandemics, meteors. He models disaster scenarios so aggressively that every offer looks suicidal. While he re-checks credit spreads, the property trades twice and cash flows for someone else. Achilles sulked in anger; this investor sulks in analysis.

- **FOMO Overdrive**
  The syndicator watching rival firms post ribbon-cutting selfies pounces on the first retail strip that hits his inbox—skipping soil reports, inflating exit cap assumptions—because not closing something feels like career death.

- **Anger Retaliation**
  A builder stiffed by an inspector stamps "never again" across his heart and deliberately lowballs every subsequent city review. Permits stall, investors sue, and the grudge kills more equity than the original insult. Achilles at least hurt foes; this anger hurts friends.

- **Prestige Addiction**
  A family office wants a trophy. The address must dazzle donors and shoulder its way onto magazine covers. Underwriting becomes pageantry; losses become sunk cost "marketing." Homer would hear echoes of Paris choosing Helen because she glittered more than a stable

throne.

Whenever numbers bend around feelings, underwriting ceases to be risk management and becomes mythmaking—tragic in the Greek sense, because the ending is foretold the moment a hero mistakes mood for metric.

Anatomy of an Emotional Hijack

Neuroscientists map emotional hijack to the amygdala, a walnut-sized cluster that launched adrenaline long before humans formed LLCs. The amygdala's signal shortcuts rational cortex loops, preparing the body for fight or flight. In the Bronze Age, that wiring dodged spears. In a closing call, it dodges reason. Heart rate climbs, palms sweat, tunnel vision narrows on the insult or threat.

Achilles illustrates the physiological pivot: his chest heaves, knuckles whiten on the sword hilt, eyes "blazing like live coals." Athena herself must descend, invisible to others, and grip his hair to keep him from murdering Agamemnon on the spot.

> "Down the goddess swept—her gray eyes blazing—
> and seized the son of Peleus by his golden hair
> only Achilles saw her, none of the rest."

Investors lack divine guardians, so they need protocols—habits as mechanical as a seat belt—that prevent the amygdala from steering the transaction. That is where the pre-offer stress test and decision log enter.

The Pre-Offer Stress Test

A pre-offer stress test is a ritual, executed before you draft an LOI, designed to surface hidden emotion and force deliberate thought. It has three stages: isolate, interrogate, and recalibrate.

1. Isolate

Step away from screens, ring tones, and team chatter. Carve twenty minutes alone with the deal memo. The goal is sensory downshift: slow breathing, steady pulse, widen awareness beyond the shiny pro-forma.

Ask: *What do I feel when I imagine winning this asset? What do I feel when I imagine losing it?* If words like *vindicated, humiliated, finally respected,* or *left behind* appear, emotion is already fingerprinting numbers. Name the feeling; writing it on paper converts vapor to object.

2. Interrogate

Open the underwriting model. For each major input—rent growth, vacancy, cap rate—write a miniature narrative: *Why do I believe this number? Which market report or firsthand data supports it? What happens if it is wrong by twenty percent?*

Then pose the key emotional check: *Would I still submit this offer if no one ever knew I owned the property?* Stripping prestige neutralizes ego. Follow with the inverse: *If a respected rival bought it at this price tomorrow, would I lose sleep?* Expose FOMO. Finally: *If an economic shock hit next quarter, would I regret leverage terms more than missing the deal?* Probe fear.

3. Recalibrate
 Adjust assumptions toward conservatism until the deal still works or breaks. If minor shifts wreck returns, the underwrite is fragile—likely propped up by feeling. Sometimes recalibration shrinks offer price. Sometimes it aborts the pursuit. Either outcome is cheaper than fury after close.

Perform the stress test aloud with a colleague if possible. Speaking claims summons counter-questions that silent reading glosses over. In Homeric councils warriors debated under open sky so the crowd could call hubris by name. Do likewise.

The Decision Log

A decision log is Achilles' shield for the modern operator—reflective bronze that shows motives back to the wielder. It is a chronological file—digital or leather bound—where every pivotal choice earns a timestamp, rationale, and data snapshot.

Structure

1. **Date/Time**

2. **Decision Node** (Submit LOI, accept appraisal shortfall, green-light CapEx change)

3. **Data Inputs** (Rent comp set, lender term sheet, engineering report)

4. **Primary Emotion Detected** (None, excitement, fear, frustration)

5. **Chosen Action**

6. **Reason in 50 Words**

7. **Forward Checkpoint** (When will I revisit outcome?)

The brevity rule forces clarity. Fifty words cannot hide self-deception. Over a portfolio's life, the log becomes a mirror. You will see patterns: always optimistic on suburban retail, always timid during election years, always pushing leverage when peers highlight trophy deals on podcasts.

Achilles lacked such a ledger; had he reread the moment he swore to sit out the war, he might have realized that pride made him hostage to a single grievance.

> "There he sat in anger, nursing his fury.
> Day after day he wasted in his ships,
> the swift sure-footed Myrmidons idle at his side."

Your capital cannot idle so long.

Case Study One: The Overbid Renovator

Madison bought three duplexes in a working-class corridor. Her first two flips had cleared sixty-five thousand dollars apiece, and podcasts invited her to speak on "scaling with velocity." When a twelve-unit block hit market, she decided it *had* to be hers. The underwriting penciled at a six-percent return after rehab—low for the neighborhood—but everyone she admired started with thin deals, right?

She skipped the pre-offer stress test, ignored the contractor's caution that cast-iron stacks might crumble, and justified a rent premium because "millennials love exposed brick." She clinched the property by adding twenty-five thousand over asking.

Eight months later, excavated plumbing revealed full line replacement; interest rates ticked up; comparable rent growth plateaued. Net return evaporated. In her autopsy she discovered she never wrote down *why* she believed tenants would value the brick, nor how fragile the budget was to contingency costs. Ego in the model, silence in the log.

Case Study Two: The Frozen Syndicator

Evan raised four million in commitments but watched the macro headwinds. He clipped newsletters from bearish economists: inverted yield curve, tightening spreads, geopolitical shocks. He ran downside scenarios so punishing that the return dipped negative under every stress. He concluded there was "no responsible entry point."

Twelve months later the same submarket posted a five-percent bump in effective rents; three deals he rejected sold at a premium. Investors, tired of holding idle funds, withdrew. Evan's fear masqueraded as prudence. The decision log—had it existed—would show a twelve-entry loop where new macro headlines trumped hard property performance stats. Data was collected but emotion picked the data to believe.

Underwriting Disciplines That Tame Emotion

1. **Blind Comp Pairs**
    Assign a partner to gather rent comps without telling you the addresses. Underwrite on square footage, vintage, and amenity only. Reveal addresses afterward. This sidelines neighborhood bias.

2. **Hard Stops on Leverage**
    Choose a maximum loan-to-value ratio on January 1 and tattoo it into policy. When brokers whisper "creative structures," your own pre-committed rulebook answers for you.

3. **Weighted Probability Outcomes**
    Model three scenarios—base, downside, upside—and assign probabilities you publicly defend. The math forces you to price in bad news instead of burying it in tab notes you never open.

4. **Third-Party Devil's Advocate**
    Pay a peer firm or mentor a flat fee to shoot holes in your package. Fire them if they ever go easy.

5. **Cooling-Off Window**
    After drafting an LOI, wait twenty-four hours. Sleep resets

amygdala sensitivity. Many an Achilles might have slept off the sword impulse.

6. **Post-Mortem Rituals**
    Schedule debriefs for closed, failed, and passed deals alike. Extract emotional fingerprints: "Did we override red flags because seller was famous?" "Did fear of litigation blind us to 1031 exit value?"

Emotional Vocabulary for Investors

Words shape feelings; refined vocabulary refines reaction. In camp the Greeks had bards to name sorrow, shame, and honor. Modern investors should cultivate language to pinpoint emotional weather:

- **Eustress** – productive tension that sharpens focus

- **Cognitive Dissonance** – discomfort when reality jars with narrative

- **Loss Aversion** – tendency to overprotect current stake versus equally sized gains

- **Narrative Fallacy** – tempting storylines distorting data interpretation

- **Herd Bias** – reflex to imitate peer behavior without independent validation

Writing any of these in the decision log pulls emotion from the subconscious into daylight, where reason can interrogate it.

Achilles' Redemption Arc: Return Without Hubris

Ultimately Achilles reenters battle not because his pride is soothed but because Patroclus dies. Grief overrides ego. He recognizes the cost of his sulk and suits up. Yet Homer grants him a moment of clarity:

> "Fate is the same for the man who holds back,
> the same if he fights hard.
> We are all held in a single honor,
> the brave with the weak and coward.
> Every mortal tastes death."

He sees that honor pursued without perspective equals death. Perspective is his late-won emotional discipline. Investors should win it sooner and cheaper.

Action Summary

- **Pre-Offer Stress Test** — twenty-minute ritual to isolate feelings, interrogate assumptions, and recalibrate numbers.

- **Decision Log** — running file of every pivotal choice with timestamp, emotion tag, and fifty-word rationale.

- **Discipline Tools** — blind comp pairs, leverage caps, weighted scenarios, devil's advocate, cooling-off window, post-mortems.

- **Vocabulary Upgrade** — adopt precise terms to label bias and emotion.

Closing Charge

Homer's genius is the warning that unchecked emotion scales catastrophe. Achilles' rage burns ships; our unexamined pride burns equity. His eventual insight—hard-won, sorrow-crusted—is free to us if we write it today inside our underwriting playbooks: *Feel, but do not obey, the first flare of emotion. Nail it to paper, sand its edges with data, and choose forward with sight restored.*

Stake that line above your monitor. When the next deal glitters like immortal glory or snarls like personal insult, pause. Breathe. Open the stress test. Write in the log. Then decide. The war will still rage outside, but inside you, the shield will hold.

Chapter 3 — The Oath of the Achaeans (Investment Thesis)

The Scene Beside the Ships

Before the first spear shuddered against Troy's walls, the Greek captains stood ankle-deep in sand and raised their hands to the morning light. They slaughtered bulls to seal a pact, poured wine in a trough of shields, and swore an oath that none would sail home until the city fell and Helen walked back beneath their banners. It was raw theater—smoke of fat on the breeze, salt spray, gulls shrieking overhead—but the ritual locked fifty quarreling kings into one outcome.

> "We will not break these oaths, but keep them truly,
> till Ilios falls and her people bow beneath us."

That sentence, uttered by Agamemnon and echoed by every ally, accomplished more than a hundred strategy councils. It clarified purpose, synchronized timelines, and gave each contingent a reason to bleed. From that hour, all tactics, all logistics, every personal feud and private ambition bent toward a single end: the breaching of Troy.

Two timeless insights live in that dawn vow. First, coalitions out-perform individuals only when the goal is unmistakable. Second, clarity requires trimming away what is merely attractive until only what is essential remains. The Greeks did not pledge "to punish Troy if convenient" or "to fight bravely until we tire." They encoded success in fourteen syllables: *till Ilios falls*. Measure effort, morale, and progress against that one line and disorder shrinks.

Modern investors assemble their own micro-coalitions—equity partners, lenders, brokers, property managers—but many never draft an oath. They talk about "value-add multifamily" on one call, "light industrial flex" on the next, chase cap rates in six metros, and tape vision statements to the office wall that do not survive the first hot lead from a persuasive broker. Their teams follow notions, not instructions, and execution scatters.

The remedy is an investment thesis just as plain, just as binding, as the Achaean oath. It is the spoken—and written—boundary within which every acquisition either clearly fits or clearly fails. Get it right and every stakeholder can tell at a glance why the deal is in the kill zone or why it belongs to someone else.

Why A Thesis Beats Talent

Numbers, contacts, capital—even courage—fail without a headline objective. Achilles proves this early. His skill is unmatched, but until his rage realigns with the coalition purpose, he is a stranded asset—swift, lethal, idle. Conversely, a middling warrior like Ajax, whose brute reliability aligns perfectly with the siege plan, matters more day-to-day. Skill plus clarity triumphs over genius unmoored.

In real estate, talent shows up as proprietary deal flow, underwriting fluency, or renovation savvy. But if those skills spray across unrelated property types, lenders hesitate, equity partners discount projections, and ops teams drown in context switching. A clear thesis gives permission to say no fast, redirect energy, and deepen expertise where returns compound.

Carving the Buy-Box

The buy-box is the physical echo of the oath—a description of the exact assets you will pursue and, by exclusion, the assets you will ignore. It limits geography, vintage, size, price band, risk profile, and operational complexity. Defining it is less about prediction than about identity: Who are you in the marketplace? Which problems are you best built to solve? Every layer you add narrows the field until the remaining targets light up like beacons.

Geography. The Greeks ringfenced their campaign to a single city. You might restrict yours to a fifty-mile radius inside a fast-growing MSA or to secondary markets within a state where legislation favors landlords. Geography multiplies advantages: local data asymmetry, vendor relationships, and political goodwill.

Asset class. Pick one and wed it. An oath that flirts with every headline trend wobbles. If you know workforce multifamily, own the segment. If you engineer cold-storage logistics, chase warehouses, not senior housing.

Vintage and construction type. A 1960s garden apartment and a 2015 podium mid-rise share rent checks but demand different cap-ex, zoning knowledge, and insurance calculus. Omit the build eras that outstrip your repair playbook.

Unit count or square footage. Scale governs financing options and operational leverage. Some funds weaponize ten-unit walk-ups because mom-and-pop sellers misprice them; others hunt 200-unit behemoths to attract institutional debt. Mixing those tiers fractures processes.

Yield profile. Are you harvesting stabilized income or forcing appreciation through heavy repositioning? Troy was a long, brutal value-add, not a coupon clipper. Define which slog you accept.

When each criterion snaps into place, you possess a buy-box. Put it in writing. Recite it when brokers call. Publish it in offering memoranda. Let friends tease you for tunnel vision; focus compounds.

Framing the Exit Horizon

An oath without a timeline is wishful thinking. The Achaeans declared *till Ilios falls*—not *for as long as it feels good*. In investment language, they set a success trigger, not a calendar date; but either form guards discipline. Days stretched into ten grinding years, yet the exit remained binary: city standing, oath alive; city burning, oath fulfilled. Because the event was external and verifiable, no king could claim premature victory.

You need the same closure mechanism. Choose either a date range ("five- to seven-year hold") or a milestone ("refinance once value reaches X" or "sell when NOI climbs to Y"). Commit publicly. Investors relax when they see a clock; lenders underwrite when they see a road map; operators budget cap-ex when they see a payout horizon. Most important, you, the sponsor, can weigh mid-campaign temptations—unsolicited offers, shiny refinance terms—against the covenant you swore.

Drafting the One-Page Investment Charter

Brevity is power. The oath that fused fifty kingdoms onto one cause fit inside a chanted stanza. Your charter must equal that economy. One sheet forces ruthless prioritization; any longer invites loopholes.

Heading. State the name of the vehicle or team and the date the charter takes effect. It is not a memo; it is a contract with yourself.

Mission Statement (One Sentence). Example: "Acquire and operate 1970-1999 vintage, 50-150 unit workforce multifamily properties within the Austin-San Antonio corridor to deliver durable cash flow and forced appreciation through operational upgrades and energy-efficient retrofits."

That sentence is a sword swipe. Everything outside its arc is someone else's war.

Buy-Box Bullets (Five Max).

1. Geography: counties or ZIP codes.

2. Asset class & vintage.

3. Minimum going-in cap rate or cash-on-cash target.

4. Acceptable occupancy band at acquisition.

5. Leverage ceiling.

Stop at five. If you need more, the idea isn't tight enough.

Exit Framework (Two Lines).
Target Hold: five years with option to exit earlier if unlevered IRR exceeds fifteen percent.
Trigger Event: refinance or sale once stabilized occupancy > 95 % for three consecutive months and market cap rates compress below five percent.

Risk Guardrails (Three Sentences).
Cap-ex reserve at close equals minimum $1,500 per unit. Floating debt hedged with rate cap to maturity plus one-year tail. Any single vendor contract above $100,000 requires dual bids.

Accountability & Updates (Two Sentences).
Charter reviewed annually every January; revisions require unanimous GP vote and written notice to LPs. Quarterly memo to stakeholders will measure actual KPIs versus charter targets.

Print, sign, countersign with your partners, and pin a copy where you underwrite.

How the Charter Filters Noise

Brokers will test boundaries. "What about this 30-unit motel conversion?" The charter answers: unit count wrong, asset wrong, next. A lender will hype eighty-five percent leverage. The charter answers: above ceiling, pass. A viral headline predicts suburban flight; the charter answers: geography unchanged unless annual review compels data-driven amendment. Each rejection saves hours, potentially months, of cognitive drag and due-diligence expense.

Just as vital, the charter deflects internal drift. When a partner suggests diversifying into self-storage "just this once," the oath hangs between you. *Till Ilios falls.* The city is still standing; stay on the wall.

Stories from the Field

The Opportunist Without a Creed. Clara ran small syndications in three states. She bought urban triplexes, suburban offices, and rural RV pads because each looked good in isolation. In year four she struggled: lenders wanted a unified pipeline, property managers had no economies, investors lost track of metrics. Cash flow met projections on some assets but underperformed on others, and her brand blurred. Had she fixed a thesis—say, class-B multifamily in tertiary Texas markets—she might have traded marginal deals for operational mastery.

The Zealous Specialist. Darius wrote a one-page charter focused on pre-1980 brick multifamily inside one county ringed by oil refineries. He liked the steady workforce and zoning inertia. Brokers protested there were only nine such properties, but he stood firm, learned every owner's anniversary, and mailed letters quarterly. Two years later, when an estate sale surfaced, he owned insider rapport and seized the asset off-market. Because his buy-box was narrow, his underwriting template was bulletproof, lenders pre-approved, and the renovation playbook reusable. NOI doubled in eighteen months. Clarity beat breadth.

When to Amend the Oath

The Greeks lost comrades, ships, and morale, yet they never edited their promise. An investment thesis, unlike their war vow, operates inside fluctuating macro cycles. Amendments can be rational—if data proves assumptions obsolete. But the bar must be high:

- **Structural market change.** Legislation caps rent increases or abolishes favorable tax abatements in your county. The geography clause might shift.

- **Capital formation shift.** You close a new fund triple the equity of the last; your minimum efficient deal size grows.

- **Technological disruption.** Energy costs spike or smart-home platforms drive renter preferences to newer stock only.

Any amendment demands the same ceremony as the original charter: draft, deliberate, unanimous consent, written notice. Casual tweaks cheapen discipline.

Measure motives ruthlessly. Are you changing the thesis because the thesis no longer works—or because a seductive deal lies five degrees outside the perimeter? If temptation drives the pen, remember Paris chose Helen despite prophecy; expedience rarely outshouts destiny.

Embedding the Oath in Daily Workflow

1. **Underwriting Checklist.** Top line reads: "Does this deal meet charter?" If no, stop.

2. **Kickoff Meeting Agenda.** The first slide after the title is the charter mission statement.

3. **Shared Drive.** The charter PDF sits in the root folder titled "Oath—Do Not Alter."

4. **Performance Dashboards.** KPIs align with buy-box metrics: average cash-on-cash, leverage ratio, occupancy trend—all benchmarked against charter targets.

5. **Quarterly Investor Calls.** Lead with charter compliance before financials. Stakeholders trust consistency.

Over time, repetition sanctifies the oath. Team members quote clauses casually: "We can't lever past seventy-five—charter line-three." That cultural shorthand is the modern echo of campfires where kings recited: *till Ilios falls.*

Speaking the Oath to External Partners

Just as Agamemnon rallied allies with clarity, you must preach your thesis to capital markets. Equity wants to hear you are not wandering. Debt wants to see risk contained. Use the one-page charter as a leave-behind after pitch meetings. Its brevity signals confidence; its specificity signals competence. The best partners self-select in: "We like your lane," or bow out: "Not our mandate." Either outcome accelerates alignment.

Guarding Against Thesis Drift During Boom Cycles

In Homer's camp, years of stalemate bred fatigue. Captains murmured about sailing home. Odysseus cracked the whip of shame to restore purpose. In a modern boom, prices bloat and the path to yield narrows. Sponsors whisper about "getting creative": ground-up condos, crypto-themed co-living, overseas resorts. The buy-box looks tight, maybe suffocating. But internally, know this: discipline feels restrictive precisely when it is most needed. Markets where every asset appears to pencil hide leverage mines and pricing cliffs. A stiff thesis forces patience until froth subsides.

Emotional Benefits of the Charter

Earlier we studied Achilles' rage. Clarity curbs emotion by replacing desire with criteria. When a broker inflates urgency—"Another buyer is circling"—you glance at the charter: occupancy too low, pass. Fear of missing out dissolves. When ego nudges you toward a skyscraper trophy, the charter asks for vintage and cap rate, not skyline photographs. Pride deflates. In this way, the oath not only coordinates strategy; it polices psychology.

A Modern Oath—Spoken Version

Stand with your partners one quiet morning, physical charter in hand, and speak the mission aloud. Voices give words weight. Something changes when lungs push air through vowels: intent crystallizes. Use ritual. Light a candle, ring a gong, whatever suits your culture, but enact the moment. State together:

"We pledge to acquire and operate only those assets that fit this charter, and to hold each other to account until our purpose is achieved."

No bulls need die, no gods descend, but the act marks the pivot from aspiration to covenant.

Action Steps Recap

1. **Draft the Charter.** One printed page; nail mission, buy-box, exit, guardrails, accountability.

2. **Sign and Store.** Ink signatures; archive digital copy where everyone sees it.

3. **Announce to Market.** Share publicly with brokers, lenders, investors; embed in pitch decks.

4. **Enforce at Intake.** First screening question on every teaser: charter fit? yes/no.

5. **Review Annually.** Schedule January session; require unanimous GP vote to amend.

6. **Narrate Often.** Begin ops meetings, investor calls, and onboarding sessions with charter slide or excerpt.

7. **Celebrate Compliance.** When a lucrative off-box deal is declined, log the event, and toast the discipline.

Closing Reflection

"Bind yourselves with this oath, mighty Argives,
so posterity will say we fought with single purpose."

The Greeks etched their place in legend by promising one thing and enduring every hardship to keep that promise. Real-estate investors write smaller legends—measured in doors, square feet, and distributions—but the moral arc is identical. Swear a thesis, keep it, and let your results rise like smoke signals across the market sky: these are the builders who know exactly why they fight and exactly when the war is won.

Chapter 4 — The Duel of Paris and Menelaus (Target Selection)

Hero versus Suitor: Why the Duel Even Matters

The armies stand stalled between city wall and surf, each side itching for a shortcut to end the siege. Paris, prince of high-towered Troy, steps forward in armor polished like a mirror. He issues a challenge to any Argive who dares to fight "for Helen and the gold." Fame, thrill, and vanity drip from every syllable. Menelaus—older, scarred, driven less by show than by contract—accepts.

> "But godlike Alexandros, fair-haired Helen's lord,
> strode out in shining mail, flaunting long plumed helm,
> and all the Trojans shuddered as he cried for single combat."

Paris chooses this showdown because it gleams, not because he can win. He enjoys archery and ambush, not heavy infantry duels. Faced with a brawny spearman, he blanches.

> "Seeing Menelaus, the dear son of Atreus,
> Paris felt his proud heart faint; back he slipped
> into the file of comrades, shrinking from death."

Aphrodite's later interference—snatching him from Menelaus' grip in a swirl of mist—exposes the imbalance further: gods rescue the unprepared, but allies and investors rarely do. In tactical terms, Paris selected the wrong target.

Menelaus, by contrast, accepts because victory lines up with capability and mission. He knows short-sword grappling, carries a balanced spear, and years of phalanx drill have hardened his wrists and lungs. The duel plays to his edge. He places commitment exactly where advantage and objective overlap.

Turning Homer into Deal Discipline

Real-estate investors parade through similar crossroads. Every teaser in the inbox is a shining prince offering glory: downtown micro-units, short-term rental resorts, co-warehousing, medical office conversions, solar-powered mobile-home parks. Each tantalizes with fresh-buzz language—cap-rate compression, institutional exit, crypto tenants—yet not every duel is winnable. The Paris problem reappears whenever a sponsor lunges at a deal whose demands do not sync with their talent stack, capital stack, or operational network.

Indicators You're About to Fight Paris-Style

- **You lead with marketing photos, not financials.**
  Paris dresses for the runway; Menelaus studies kill zones. If listing pictures dominate your excitement, you are following polish, not probability.

- **The underwriting model relies on best-case timelines you have never met.**
  Paris imagines a quick kill and triumphant parade; actual sieges grind. Extrapolated perfection is fantasy.

- **Your key vendors are "sure they can figure it out."**
  Paris relies on divine bailout. Menelaus trains with men who can wield shields in their sleep. Vendors learning on your dime equal risk.

- **The risk memo begins with "Everyone's doing this now."**
  That is herd momentum, not asymmetric advantage.

Payoffs of Menelaus-Style Targeting

- **Quick conviction or quick pass.**
  When you know your weapon—say, workforce multifamily inside C-class garden walk-ups—you see fit or misfit within minutes, sparing diligence spend.

- **Pricing power.**
  Niche mastery surfaces warts competing bidders miss: easement oddities, submetering opportunities, code grandfather clauses. You bake fixes into your offer while rivals either overpay or walk.

- **Operational compounding.**
  Same boiler spec, same turn-grade flooring, same tax argument letter copy from deal to deal. Learning curves

flatten; margins widen.

Anatomy of a Targeting Philosophy

1. **Capability Alignment**
   What tasks can you or your direct hires perform
   unconsciously well? Menelaus knows shield wall timing;
   you might know Class-B leasing negotiation, or distressed
   note acquisition. Skill is the core.

2. **Resource Certainty**
   Do you command the capital, credit, and contractor depth
   sized to the asset? Fighting with half-shod sandals invites
   heel wounds.

3. **Information Edge**
   Achilles swings a bronze-bladed spear none can match;
   your edge might be granular census tract rent data or
   zoning lawyer retainer. If the duel does not leverage some
   edge, it's Parisian vanity.

4. **Strategic Relevance**
   Does the battle move you toward your previously sworn
   thesis? A trophy duel outside the campaign arc drains
   focus.

The sweet spot where all four rings overlap reveals *winnable*
targets. Everything else carries divine-rescue risk.

From War Stories to Deal Flow: Building the Deal-Fit Matrix

Paris and Menelaus teach through contrast. To mechanize their lesson, build a decision tool that screens opportunities against capability and thesis with brutal speed. A *deal-fit matrix* does precisely that.

Core Axes

- **Vertical Axis: Capability Fit**
  Score each incoming deal on a scale from natural mastery (top) to steep, expensive learning curve (bottom).

- **Horizontal Axis: Strategic Fit**
  Score from perfect alignment with charter (left) to off-mission shiny object (right).

Plot the opportunity. The upper-left quadrant is Menelaus country: engage. Lower-right is Paris territory: disengage. The other two quadrants invite cautious thought or partnership structuring.

Practical Construction

1. **List Capabilities and Constraints.**
   Write short statements: "We have on-call crews for 1980s plumbing," "We lack cold-storage HVAC expertise," "Equity expects yield within eighteen months," "Permitting counsel

is fluent in City A, not City B."

2. **Choose Five Binary Questions for Each Axis.**
   Examples for Capability

   - Do we have a vendor proven on this asset type?

   - Is funding for purchase and stabilization pre-committed?

   - Can our existing management platform absorb without retool?

   - Have we executed a similar scope within the past twenty-four months?

   - Is the location within our routine travel footprint?

3. Examples for Strategic

   - Does the asset fall inside charter geography?

   - Does the business plan mirror our established risk band?

   - Does the projected hold window fit LP expectations?

   - Is required leverage $\leq$ charter ceiling?

- Will exit comparables validate value on current market norms?

4. Each *yes* equals one point. Five points per axis.

5. **Score Live.**
   During the first read of a deal package, tick boxes. Capability four, Strategic two? Mathematically that lands left center-low—still Paris risk. Only four-plus on both axes merits full diligence.

6. **Record and Review.**
   Keep matrix plots in a shared drive. Patterns will emerge: maybe suburban flex drops Strategic scores; maybe heavy-rehab vintage hits Capability lows. **Learn** where weakness repeats and either build capability or contract target scope.

7. **Institutionalize**
   Require matrix completion before green-lighting third-party reports or hard deposit. Discipline up front saves six-figure dead-deal costs.

The Role of Ego and Narrative in Target Drift

Paris' fatal misread stems from story addiction. He sees himself a glittering champion beloved of Aphrodite; he broadcasts that narrative until it rewires risk perception. In modern underwriting, story gets laundered as "thesis expansion." Listen for these signs:

- "We've done great in workforce multifamily, so student housing shouldn't be too different."

- "Our GC nailed the last 40-unit, so a ground-up 200-unit is the next logical evolution."

- "The LPs keep asking for bigger deals; this lifestyle co-living campus will wow them."

Notice how each pitch starts with *We have momentum*, not *We have new mastery.* Narrative streaks ahead of competency. The cure is the matrix—cold squares trump bright adjectives.

Partnering to Borrow Competence

Sometimes a duel lies just outside your left-upper quadrant but holds strategic synergy if skills can be rented. Menelaus did not borrow Paris' bow; but Grecian heroes frequently combined talent—Odysseus devising strategy while Diomedes executed night raids. Investors may likewise joint-venture:

- **Fee for Service.** Bring in a management firm with deep student-housing playbooks while you supply capital and acquisitions finesse.

- **Structured Co-GP.** Exchange equity for expertise: fifty-fifty with a ground-up specialist while you contribute local entitlements relationships.

- **Board of Advisers.** Pay retainers to seasoned pros who review budgets and site plans weekly. Cheaper than salvage.

Partnership, however, only shifts a lower Capability score to neutral if well-structured. It cannot drag a Strategic misfit leftward. If a deal tags the right edge of the matrix, partnership is lipstick on the prince.

Case Illustration: The Nine-Acre Mirage

A broker pitched a riverfront parcel zoned for mixed-use luxury condos plus retail. Pictures boasted glass turrets, café terraces, kayak docks. The sponsor specialized in B-class garden apartments an hour inland. In the matrix:

- Capability: vendor crew had zero high-rise experience (0), construction loan relationships thin (0), management unfamiliar with condo docs (0), miles beyond travel ring (0), but equity could stretch (1). Capability score: 1.

- Strategic: geography outside charter (0), asset class foreign (0), hold window uncertain (0), leverage heavy (0), potential IRR attractive (1). Strategic score: 1.

1×1 plot: far-low-right. Sponsor declined in forty-five minutes, saved months of architect fees, and closed a bread-and-butter twenty-unit instead.

Tactical Zoom: Running the Matrix on a Live Call

Picture the deal team on Zoom, PDFs open.

"First question," the acquisitions lead asks, "Inside or outside our two-county footprint?"

"Inside," analyst replies. Tick strategic point.

"Existing crew know this HVAC system?"

"No—chiller-tower, we've never maintained one."

Capability zero.

"Occupancy?"

"Ninety-two; light value-add."

Capability one; strategic one. They push on. By the tenth question totals read Capability four, Strategic four—upper-left. Move to LOI.

Time elapsed: seven minutes. Energy preserved for deals worth sieging.

Emotional Hygiene: Saying No Politely but Finally

Greek heroes seldom declined a fight; honor ranked higher than prudence. Modern investors must reverse the order. Your NO should be crisp enough to end loop conversations yet courteous enough to preserve deal flow. Script:

"Thanks for thinking of us. After a quick fit analysis, this asset sits outside our current mandate because [one sentence reason pulled from matrix]. Let's regroup when you have a [descriptor inside charter]."

Clear, specific, and door-keeping.

Integrating Matrix Output with the Investment Charter

The charter, forged in Chapter 3, states mission. The matrix tests each prospective battle against that mission's realities. Over time, feedback loops tighten both documents. If matrix rejection rate in a focus county runs eighty-percent due to Capability gaps, maybe the charter over-promised; either bolster crews or adjust geography.

Conversely, if ninety-percent of passes track to Strategic misfit and only ten-percent to Capability, the world keeps dangling shiny objects—you are refusing wisely. Celebrate the discipline.

When to Override the Matrix

Great commanders bend rules only under exceptional alignment of reward and available margin for error. Criteria:

- **Outlier Return Compensates Complexity.** A thirty-percent unlevered IRR can justify building a new skill, if risk is containable.

- **De-Risking Partnerships Secure Missing Capability.** Co-GP carries deep guarantees and aligned exit.

- **Mission Revision Under Due Process.** The charter is formally amended, not casually skirted. The duel becomes new doctrine, not aberration.

Make sure overrides are logged. Every mythic tragedy begins with leaders believing exceptions exempt them from fate.

Paris, Menelaus, and the Investor's Mindset

After Aphrodite spirits Paris away, Homer offers a last word:

> "War-loving Menelaus ranged up and down the lines
> like a wild beast, seeking godlike Paris.
> But none of the Trojans, none of their famous allies,
> could show him where he moved."

The Trojans hide their prince because morale would collapse if the army saw how fragile its champion truly was. Markets likewise conceal the pain of sponsors who charged into misfit assets; bad numbers hide until capital calls arrive. Menelaus, though bloodied, walks tall among troops, proof that choosing the right duel allows a clean conscience win or lose. Investors who select battles aligned with skill and thesis may still fight hard markets, but dignity and probability stand guard.

Step-By-Step Action Plan

1. **Define Matrix Questions.** Draw from skill inventory, charter, and vendor depth. Keep each binary.

2. **Set Passing Thresholds.** Decide—four-plus on each axis moves to LOI; three or fewer kills.

3. **Automate in CRM.** Embed the questionnaire so every lead captures scores.

4. **Train the Team.** Role-play till analysts can score without hesitation.

5. **Track Outcomes.** Post-mortem closed deals: did matrix predict performance? Adjust weights.

6. **Review Quarterly.** Capability growth may shift some zeros to ones; update.

7. **Log Overrides.** If a partner insists on pursuing a low-score target, document rationale, timeframe, guardrails.

Closing Image

See Paris in silks, smiling for the crowd, unaware he is moments from the spear point of a grim Spartan king. See Menelaus heft his shield, not flamboyant, just certain. In the hush before first clang, one duelist chases applause; the other, outcome.

Choose your properties the way Menelaus chooses opponents—where your range, reach, and resolve give you the statistical edge. Draw the matrix. Trust its verdict. The sand of Ilium is littered with princes who mistook shine for strength. Your investors deserve fewer monuments to vanity, more forts won by craft.

Chapter 5 — Helen's Face (Compelling Deals)

1. Wind on the Ramps: Why One Woman Was Worth Ten Years

When Priam's scouts first spotted the Greek armada, the beach darkened with ships "as many as leaves or sands." A thousand prows knifed into the surf because one Spartan queen crossed the Aegean under Trojan escort. The price of recovering Helen was ruinous: fathers and sons abandoned farms, kings pledged gold they did not have, bronze melted into spearheads by the ton. Why pour lifetimes into a single retrieval? Because—right or wrong—every captain believed the prize would rewrite destiny.

> "Like the sudden flare of a beacon burning from isle to isle
> announcing war, so shone Helen's beauty under Troy's sun."

Beauty in Homer is shorthand for unique, non-replicable value. Helen is scarce; her capture humiliates an empire and her return promises reputational windfall. That asymmetry—gigantic upside for the holder, catastrophic loss for the loser—justifies a siege no accountant would otherwise sign off. In modern capital markets, compelling deals carry the same magnetism. They bend schedules, budgets, even alliances, because what they yield can change the scale or brand of an entire portfolio.

2. Trophy Assets versus Yield Plays

A trophy asset is a Helen: singular, scarce, emotionally resonant, politically symbolic. Think of the pre-war Art Deco tower on a skyline postcard, the marina-front parcel with perpetual riparian rights, the landmark warehouse that anchors an emerging life-sciences cluster. Buy one and your business card reads differently the next morning. LPs return calls faster; banks waive covenants; coverage in glossy magazines blurs into free advertising. Trophy assets create reputational equity, a currency you can spend for decades.

Yield plays are Menelaus' cattle herds—unromantic, steady, vital. Twelve-unit walk-ups, flex industrial boxes, garden apartments on commuter beltlines: they feed distributions and recycle cash, but few investors frame them on office walls. Yield plays compound wealth quietly; trophies ignite brand and optionality. Knowing which hunt you are on changes every tactic.

Key contrasts in plain language

- **Scarcity.** There will always be another eight-cap duplex; there may never be another flatiron corner zoned for twenty stories with a river view.

- **Liquidity Curve.** Trophy assets boast eager buyer pools even in recessions; yield plays rely on cash-flow math and debt availability.

- **Holding Cost Tolerance.** You can weather longer vacancies on a landmark if long-run appreciation dwarfs interim pain. Yield plays must cash-flow quickly or your IRR evaporates.

- **Stakeholder Psychology.** Investors thrill at owning a marquee hotel in Miami Beach, even at a slimmer dividend; they judge a Class-C motel on the interstate by rent roll alone.

- **Exit Optionality.** A trophy can refinance into museum tax credits, adaptive-reuse grants, or boutique funds chasing ESG halo; yield plays exit via cap-rate compression or 1031 chains.

Neither category is superior in the abstract. A portfolio usually needs both—the reliable soldiers who hold the line and the astonishing prize that makes the war worth waging.

---

3. The Temptation Trap: Lusting After a Face without Counting the Cost

Paris never read a loan doc. He accepted Helen because desire blurred arithmetic. Kings arriving on Troy's walls soon discovered the embedded liabilities: supply shortages, plague, the wrath of Achilles. Investors too can mis-price trophies. The ease with which a golden marquee charms egos can override standard underwriting guardrails.

Symptoms of over-paying for glamour:

- Skipping third-party environmental reports because "the building is iconic."

- Justifying sub-market cash flow on the promise of tourism up-cycles tied to events four years away.

- Accepting full-recourse debt when a stabilized DSCR won't exceed 1.15 until year five.

- Ignoring warning emails from asset managers who see deterioration behind marble lobbies.

Homer slips a warning inside Helen's own lament. Standing on the wall, she reproaches Paris:

> "Would that I had died before I left my bridal chamber—
> death would have spared me this."

Even the prize may carry remorse. Ask yourself before pursuit: will this asset still look beautiful in a rising-rate drought? Will investors cherish it if distributions stall? A trophy is not an excuse for negligent math; it is a reason for disciplined, expanded diligence.

---

4. High-Stakes Campaign Math

Long wars hemorrhage treasure and morale. Yet the Greeks endured because expected payoff dwarfed sunk costs. Translate to deal structuring:

- **Time Horizon Flex.** Build contingency for entitlement delays, adaptive-reuse approvals, historic-tax-credit audits. Add twelve months to best-case and model carry cost at today's SOFR plus 400 basis points.

- **Layered Capital.** Blend patient equity (family offices hungry for brand exposure) with mezzanine willing to capitalize interest. Value accretion in a trophy often comes in one step—certificate of occupancy or landmark designation—so cash yield may wait.

- **Liquidity Backstop.** Like Greek supply ships ferrying grain, set aside revolving credit equal to at least six months of full burn (debt service plus overhead) for every one year you expect to hold.

- **Stakeholder Signaling.** Circulate quarterly narrative memos to keep morale; silence breeds mutiny when distributions pause. Invoke the vision: "We are minting the Rockefeller Center of bio-pharma labs."

Without such buffers, the siege collapses at the first plague of plagues: contractor insolvency, permit moratorium, cyber insurance shock.

5. The Value-Driver Scorecard

Helen's allure is obvious; what turns a building into Helen requires more granularity. Enter the scorecard: a written, repeatable checklist ranking qualitative and quantitative levers. Draft the template once, then grade every would-be trophy before you marshal war chests.

Intrinsic Scarcity

- Historical or architectural protection

- Irreplaceable location (waterfront, transit hub, cultural nexus)

- Zoning anomalies impossible to replicate

Market Magnetism

- Visibility index (press coverage, skyline role, tourism draw)

- Vacancy stickiness (blue-chip tenants, wait-list residential demand)

- Demographic tailwinds (STEM job growth, aging affluent populations, luxury retail appetite)

Upside Catalysts

- In-place rents versus Class-A comparables

- Ready path to higher & better use (air rights, additional FAR)

- Tax or incentive overlays (historic rehab credits, opportunity-zone equity)

Risk Dampeners

- Diverse tenancy or alternative exit verticals

- Political goodwill (city eager for redevelopment)

- Minimal environmental liabilities

Portfolio Synergy

- Brand halo effect on fundraising

- Cross-marketing with existing assets

- Tenant migration pipeline across properties

Score each sub-item from zero to three. A deal sailing above seventy percent of the total threshold moves into full-siege mode. Anything below is a beautiful face glued to cardboard armor—step back.

6. Case Study: The Sleeping Citadel

A decommissioned 1910 train station, granite colonnades and Tiffany glass, sat mothballed in a second-tier city's downtown. Three previous buyers failed: asbestos abatement sticker shock, parking variance denials, rotted utilities. Our sponsor—a midsize multifamily specialist—hesitated, but the scorecard suggested hidden gold.

- Intrinsic Scarcity: 9/9 (last Beaux-Arts station in the region)

- Market Magnetism: 6/9 (city's tourism bureau had revival plans)

- Upside Catalysts: 7/9 (air rights plus state heritage grants)

- Risk Dampeners: 5/9 (contaminants mapped, city supportive)

- Portfolio Synergy: 6/9 (could feed luxury loft pipeline)

Composite: 33/45—well above seventy percent. The sponsor partnered with a historic consultant, layered New Markets Tax Credits, and converted hall concourses into food-hall revenue at twice projected rent. Equity saw no coupon for three years; final refinance doubled basis. Patience, buttressed by the scorecard, paid mythic dividends.

7. Case Study: The Tarnished Tiara

Across the river, a glass office tower promised skyline clout. Brokers draped renderings with talk of "world-class ESG reposition." The sponsor, dazzled, submitted LOI without a scorecard pass. Six months of diligence unearthed:

- Non-divisible floor plates hindering coworking pivot

- Union elevator contracts locked at triple regional averages

- Obsolete curtain-wall failing energy code

Retrospective scoring landed below fifty percent. Earnest money vanished, internal credibility bruised. The team now prints the scorecard in bold and tapes it above the acquisition desk.

---

8. Balancing Portfolios: When Yield Should Out-vote Beauty

Achilles gleams beneath celestial armor, but the tide often turns on anonymous shield-bearers. A fund fixated on trophies risks diet imbalance: lumpy IRRs, elongated capital calls, overexposure to macro tourism shocks. Steady smaller assets buffer cash flow. They bankroll the siege.

Practical policy:

- Maintain a 60/40 split—yield assets cover pref return; trophy assets chase equity kicker.

- Use yield cash flow to self-fund trophy cap-ex, limiting dilution.

- Sunlight risky exposures in investor dashboards: "Thirty percent of capital tied in zero-yield growth tranche." Transparency inoculates against impatience.

In Homeric lines:

> "Many brave souls, their bodies left the field,
> food for dogs and birds, all for the sake of Helen."

Manage so your operation need not sacrifice too many brave souls (core assets) chasing one glittering prize.

---

9. Psychological Armor for Long Campaigns

Human stamina, not spreadsheets, decides prolonged battles. Month thirty of a landmark rehab may tempt anyone to dump at break-even. Methods to stay the course:

- **Milestone Rituals.** Celebrate each permit win, façade unveiling, anchor lease. Burnout fades when victories puncture the horizon.

- **Narrative Journaling.** Record weekly progress notes; read month-one fear entries to remember how far the siege has advanced.

- **Stakeholder Storytelling.** Tour investors through scaffolding, show artisans restoring ironwork. Tangible scenes replace dusty delays with heroic imagery.

- **Vision Re-anchoring.** Revisit charter: Why did we choose this Helen? Realign hearts before budgets.

Hector, viewing the battlefield, encouraged troops:

> "Stand firm, my friends, and think of wives and children,
> of fatherland and honor, and we shall hold the wall."

Replace "wives and children" with "cash-on-cash and legacy," and the speech fits any construction trailer at 6 a.m.

---

10. Exit Strategy: Bringing Helen Home

The Greeks won not at the duel, but at the negotiation table inside the wooden horse's aftermath. A compelling deal only crowns victory when you crystallize value:

- **Institutional Exit.** Core funds and REITs pay premiums for stabilized landmarks; underwrite building systems to their spec early.

- **Monetize Air Rights.** Retain vertical parcels; sell later to hospitality flags.

- **Sale-Leaseback with Cultural Bodies.** Museums or universities covet historic wings but prefer cap-ex free use; structure triple-net leases.

- **Convert to Fund Anchor.** Roll trophy into a new vehicle as seed, raising fresh equity on halo effect.

Always pre-write two exit playbooks—optimistic and defensive. Paris never planned for defeat; Menelaus marched with contingencies.

---

11. Crafting Your Own Helen Filter

Write these prompts on a single page:

1. Does this asset grant us a story no competitor can match?

2. Can we model break-even returns under double-long timelines and triple-wide cost overruns?

3. Which future buyers hunger for exactly this address or entitlement?

4. What permanent advantage does ownership confer beyond IRR?

5. How many routine deals must perform to subsidize the march?

Answer in ink. If blanks linger, you are wooing Helen with borrowed plumes.

---

12. Field Orders

- Draft your value-driver scorecard tonight; circulate to the team for blind scoring on two past wins and two past failures.

- Divide pipeline into trophy and yield stacks; color-code capital sources accordingly.

- Establish capital call thresholds and rotation policies to shield yield investors from trophy-driven delays.

- Plan a milestone ritual for every major entitlement or lease; book dates in advance.

- Rehearse exit narratives for any live trophy pursuit; if you cannot pitch the sequel, abandon the siege.

Closing Chorus

In the final book of the *Iliad*, Helen mourns over Hector's corpse, recognizing that the war her face ignited has devoured the greatest defender of her adoptive city. The lines tremble with remorse:

> "Never again will I find so gentle a heart in all wide Troy,
> and I shiver at the thought of the night."

Compelling prizes demand tribute—time, attention, even loss. Yet without them, history forgets names. Your investing life will accumulate many steady, honorable rents, but a few radiant assets will brand your legacy. Seek them with sobriety, siege them with patience, and score them with rigor. Let their acquisition be a song worth the years.

Chapter 6 — The Shield of Achilles (Risk Armor)

---

1. Bronze at Dawn: What the Shield Means in the *Iliad*

On the night before Achilles re-enters the war, Thetis rises from the sea and climbs the forge of Hephaestus. The smith-god, sweating celestial fire, hammers tin and gold into a disc so large two men must carry it. Homer lingers on the imagery—city at peace, city at war, fields under harvest, constellations wheeling overhead—because the shield is more than hardware; it is a cosmology cast in metal. Every layer tells Achilles the world he is about to walk into.

> "He made the earth on it, and the sky, and the sea,
>   the unwearied sun, and the moon at the full,
>   and all the constellations that crown the heavens."

In martial terms, the shield is the only thing capable of intercepting Hector's spear. In strategic terms, it is an insurance policy against variance: wind, arrows, spiteful gods. Achilles will drive forward because layers of alloy absorb shocks his flesh cannot. Without that buffer, even the greatest warrior stays in the tent.

---

2. Translating Bronze into Balance Sheets

Modern investors face arrows shaped like lawsuits, roof leaks, rate spikes, data breaches, and Acts of God. A trophy asset dazzles, a yield play feeds, but neither survives an unmitigated loss event. Risk armor, therefore, is not optional decoration; it is mandatory infrastructure.

The parallels align point for point:

- **Outer Rim – Property Insurance**

- **Second Band – Liability Shields**

- **Third Band – Contractual Hedging**

- **Fourth Band – Entity Structure**

- **Inner Core – Behavioral Discipline**

Together they form a defense-in-depth, each ring intercepting a threat category, dispersing force before it can pierce net worth.

---

3. Ring One: Property Insurance — The City at Peace

Hephaestus etches plowmen guiding oxen and vines heavy with grapes, scenes of prosperity untouched by war. This tranquility is the default state investors assume when underwriting: roofs stay watertight, tenants pay, weather cooperates. Property insurance transfers the risk that the vineyard burns.

Essential Coverages

1. Replacement-cost building coverage.

2. Business-income or loss-of-rents coverage.

3. Boiler and machinery for chiller towers, elevators, solar arrays.

4. Ordinance and law for code upgrades after partial loss.

5. Flood and quake riders if geography demands.

Premiums pinch cash flow, but unfunded rebuilds annihilate equity. One hailstorm can vaporize a decade of NOI. The shield's outer rim must be intact.

---

4. Ring Two: Liability Shields — The City at War

The next circle depicts besieging armies, ambushes in dusty ravines, families weeping on battlements. Conflict is inevitable. Your version is a tenant slip-and-fall, a subcontractor mangled on a jobsite, a carbon-monoxide leak. Liability insurance (and accompanying contractual indemnities) deflects these spears.

Key Tools

- Commercial General Liability (CGL) with high per-occurrence and aggregate limits.

- Umbrella or excess liability to extend caps into eight-figure territory.

- Environmental liability if historical dry-cleaner residue slumbers beneath asphalt.

- Director and Officer (D&O) coverage when outside investors can sue management.

Achilles' shield shows defenders forming a ring-lock phalanx. In legal life, that phalanx is a stack of endorsements, additional-insured clauses, waivers of subrogation, and explicit risk transfer in vendor agreements.

---

5. Ring Three: Contractual Hedging — Harvest Under Stars

Inside the war circle, Hephaestus engraves reapers binding wheat, singers marking time. These cyclical images remind us cash flow ebbs and flows under macro seasons beyond mortal control. Interest-rate hedging, commodity futures, and swap agreements lock portions of those seasons.

Interest-Rate Tools

- **Rate Caps.** Pay an upfront premium; counter-party covers LIBOR or SOFR above strike.

- **Swaps.** Fixed-for-floating exchange on a notional loan balance; mark-to-market risk must be collateralized.

- **Forward-Starting Swaps.** Hedge future refi environments.

- **Treasury Locks.** Secure permanent debt coupons sixty to ninety days pre-close.

Expense Hedges

- Natural-gas futures for central boilers.

- Diesel contracts for logistics assets.

- Copper futures if large-scale rewiring.

Hedging is expensive if priced in hindsight; cheap compared with busted pro-formas. The shield's harvest scenes whisper: secure the fruits of labor before frost or fire steals them.

6. Ring Four: Entity Architecture — Dancers and Laws

Closer to the shield's hub, Homer sets dancers weaving hand in hand, order amid chaos. Legal entities perform this choreography for assets: separate LLCs, master holding companies, series structures. If one entity stumbles, the rest keep tempo.

Foundational Practices

- Segregate each property into its own single-purpose entity (SPE).

- Use a holding LLC or LP to own membership interests, keeping personal assets beyond creditor reach.

- Draft operating agreements with poison-pill clauses blocking hostile takeovers.

- Layer a management company for payroll and service contracts, protecting property entities from employment lawsuits.

- In high-risk rehabs, form project LLCs that dissolve post-completion, limiting tail liability.

Arguments surface that entity layering is costly. So is a joint-and-several judgment. Structural separation is a moat; litigants must cross multiple drawbridges.

7. Ring Five: Behavioral Discipline — Constellations Overhead

The shield's center gleams with the full cosmos: Pleiades, Orion, Bear. Stars are constants against which navigators plot. A risk program dies if owners ignore its rules. Behavioral discipline is the inner bronze that no enemy can penetrate unless the carrier drops the shield.

Daily Practices

- **Gap Review Calendar.** Quarterly audits ensure coverage values track inflation and new improvements.

- **Contract Checklist.** No contractor sets foot on site without COI naming owner, lender, and PM as additional insured.

- **Counter-Signature Rule.** No refi proceeds without a new hedge quote; no JV closed without entity waterfall alignment.

- **Incident Drill.** Run tabletop exercises: pipe burst, ransomware, wrongful-death claim. Response time cements or cracks fortune.

- **Document Vault.** Cloud repository plus off-site backup retains policies, endorsements, claim photos, sworn statements—armor is useless if lost to laptop theft.

Achilles may be semi-divine, but sloppy habit kills mortals and companies alike. A forged shield left leaning in sand corrodes; bronze shines only when polished.

---

8. Identifying Gaps: The Risk-Armor Worksheet

Write on paper, one page per asset.

Section A – Hard Assets

1. When was replacement-cost appraisal last updated?

2. Does policy limit cover that value plus annual CPI?

3. Are ordinance and law endorsements equal to twenty percent of replacement?

4. Flood zone status cross-checked with most recent FEMA map?

Section B – Revenue Continuity

1. Business-income coverage length versus projected rebuild timeline?

2. Market-rent escalation riders?

3. Minimum deductible aligned with cash reserves?

Section C – Legal Shields

1. Entity chart current?

2. Out-of-state registration where property sits?

3. Operating-agreement indemnity language tested?

4. Umbrella limit matched to total portfolio equity at risk?

Section D – Financial Hedging

1. Loan covenants for mandatory caps?

2. Swap breakage scenario tested under sale?

3. Mezzanine triggers synchronized with swap maturity?

Section E – Human Process

1. Last insurance renewal audit date?

2. Vendor COI tracker up to date?

3. Crisis plan binder location?

4. Staff training session held this quarter?

Rank each answer green (secure), yellow (partial), red (gap). Sum reds. Attack highest-impact reds first: a roof without wind/hail endorsement outranks a low umbrella limit; an unhedged floating-rate bridge on $50 million outranks a missing copper hedge. Schedule mitigation timelines, responsible party, cost estimate.

---

9. Case Study: The Apartment That Survived the Twister

A 1980s, 120-unit community in Oklahoma rested under a $25 million bridge, 80 percent floating. Sponsor bought a three-year, 3-percent SOFR cap for $300 k, though peers balked at cost. Year two, a tornado shredded two buildings. Property insurance replaced structures; business-income rider paid debt service; rate cap cushioned interest surge when Fed hikes followed. Investors lost one quarter of distributions but never faced cash calls. Neighboring asset, identical vintage, lacked cap and adequate ordinance coverage; its sponsor defaulted. Armor layers matter.

---

10. Case Study: The Lawsuit That Bypassed the Shield

A self-storage operator formed individual LLCs but failed to buy umbrella coverage above $1 million. A customer injured by a faulty roll-up door sued. Jury awarded $6 million; CGL paid first million, LLC bankrupted, but attorneys pierced veil citing co-mingled vendor payments from central account. Parent company, uninsured for excess, wrote settlement checks. One missing layer—discipline—let the spear through.

---

11. Evolving Threats: New Spears on the Horizon

- **Cyber Extortion.** Smart locks and cloud PM platforms invite ransomware; cyber liability joins the CGL stack.

- **Climate Drift.** "Hundred-year" floods strike every five years; parametric insurance and micro-grid resilience become outer rims.

- **Social Inflation.** Juror sentiment pushes verdicts beyond umbrella limits; consider higher towers or captive insurance.

- **Regulation Shock.** Rent caps, gas bans, electrification mandates alter OPEX; embed political-risk insurance in certain jurisdictions.

Hephaestus' shield, if cast today, might show data streams and wildfire lines beside rivers and oxen.

---

12. Integrating Risk Armor with the Investment Thesis

The charter from Chapter 3 sets strategy; the shield supports it. A fund promising five-year holds cannot assume two-year insurance payouts. Trophy rehabs need builders-risk terms aligning with tax-credit milestones. Niche industrial portfolios riding variable leases should swap diesel futures. Armor and aim are inseparable.

---

13. Cultural Adoption: Making Risk a Team Sport

Achilles fights alone but survives through forged layers. In real life, risk culture filters through every payroll tier.

- **On-Site Managers** photograph water intrusion weekly.

- **Asset Managers** renew caps 90 days pre-expiry.

- **Controllers** reconcile insurance escrows monthly.

- **Executives** review gap worksheets quarterly and adjust strategic cash.

Celebrate staff who spot cracks—gift cards, call-outs in company town halls. Fearless whistle-points add steel to bronze.

14. Ritual of Renewal

Thetis gifts Achilles the shield at dawn. Underwriters gift renewals annually. Approach each renewal as divine visitation:

1. Update replacement-cost valuation.

2. Obtain three quotes; pressure incumbents.

3. Review loss runs; implement carrier recommendations.

4. Re-score risk worksheet; migrate new yellows to greens.

Stagnant coverage corrodes like saltwater on bronze.

---

15. Closing Invocation

> "And when Achilles lifted the great shield,
> light flashed far like the moon seen by sailors
> over open seas, whose lonely hearts are cheered."

The sight of solid defense emboldens allies—LPs, lenders, tenants. They sail with you into markets whose seas darken unpredictably. Let your armor flash reassurance. For every spear yet forged, build a layer. For every gap revealed, plate it. And march, confident that what touches you first meets bronze, not bone.

Chapter 7 — The Trojan Horse (Creative Financing)

1   Night on the Ramparts: Why Cunning Beats Catapults

For ten summers bronze crashed against the Trojan wall and broke. Agamemnon sacrificed bulls, Ajax heaved rocks, Achilles slew champions by the dozen, yet limestone towers still crowned the plain. Only when brute force exhausted itself did a different weapon appear—one made of spruce, silence, and deceit. Odysseus proposed it:

> "Friends, let us fashion a hollow horse of timber,
> huge as our longing, and hide picked men inside,
> then leave it on the strand as an offering.
> The path to victory runs not through the gate,
> but under it."

No sword changed the war so completely. Troy's elders debated, dragged the horse within their own defenses, and uncorked destruction from the inside out. Ten years of attrition surrendered to one night of imagination.

Investors confront their own high walls: appraisal gaps, seller tax liabilities, fatigued capital partners, interest-rate ceilings. Many respond by swinging bigger hammers—more equity, higher bids, shorter diligence—until returns bleed out. Better to channel

Odysseus. When the conventional door is barred, build a Trojan Horse of deal structure that walks you under the lintel while opponents sleep.

---

2 Anatomy of the Wooden Genius

The power in the horse lay not in mass but in layers of asymmetry:

- **Psychological Appeal.** The gift answered Troy's desire for omens of deliverance.

- **Resource Efficiency.** Timber came from abandoned ship timbers—cheap, repurposed.

- **Hidden Leverage.** Warriors rode the machine; energy expended once, multiplied later.

- **Timing.** Horse appeared after a false retreat, exploiting festival laxity.

- **Alignment with Enemy Incentives.** Priests argued the horse would shield the city; the very form seemed blessing, not threat.

Creative financing copies these levers. Seller carries soothe tax pain; lease-options transform reluctance into incremental rent; equity swaps transmute ill-liquidity into diversified paper. None require more brawn—just pattern insight.

3   Seller Carrybacks: Smuggling Equity Past the Gate

Picture a family that has owned a flex-industrial yard since the end of the Cold War. Their basis is peanuts; a straight sale prints a capital-gains tax large enough to fund a small regiment. You, the buyer, approach with a conventional loan and 25 percent down. Negotiations stall.

Enter the wooden horse: offer a seller-financed second mortgage or, if lender allows, a wraparound note. The family defers gain, stretches income over years, earns interest above treasury yields, and feels like they lent—not lost—their legacy. Your equity outlay drops, DSCR may rise if the carry rate beats mezz market, and your price edge over all-cash rivals narrows.

Crucial clauses:

1. **Subordination Agreement** acceptable to senior lender.

2. **Cross-default** tying any delinquency to acceleration, yet with a grace period to repair.

3. **Collateral Assignment of Rents** only after senior cure windows close.

4. **Due-on-Sale Flex** if you exit via refinance inside hold period.

The seller thinks they've walked wealth into safe harbour; in reality, you've walked a squad of capital across their ramparts.

---

4   Lease-Options: Controlling the Keep Before Owning It

Odysseus did not storm the throne room in the first hour; he waited, studied guard change, picked the moment. A lease-option agreement provides similar patience. You pay option consideration up-front—usually one to three percent of strike price—then lease the property for one to three years. During term, you:

- Renovate cosmetics under a pre-agreed scope.

- Stabilize rents, proving out projections.

- Season financials for future lenders.

- Accumulate further option credit from each rent check if negotiated.

If macro winds shift, you can decline to exercise; option fee is the sacrificed ship, not a fleet. Sellers wary of stigma from a formal listing accept because they retain title and perceived control. Meanwhile, you harvest upside akin to ownership with risk capped at option cost and cap-ex. The horse here is legal: control rights smuggled inside a tenancy cloak.

Drafting pillars:

- **Purchase Price Indexing** to a neutral benchmark (CPI plus cap-rate spread) to satisfy both parties' market fears.

- **Cap-Ex Covenants** clarifying which improvements earn reimbursement at close and which revert.

- **Performance Default Provisions**—miss two months rent, option forfeits. Clarity spares lawsuits.

- **Title Escrow** holding executed deed and releases to guarantee closing mechanics once option triggers.

Lease-options shine where credit hiccups or rate spikes momentarily hamstring senior debt. They also court 1031 sellers who need tax timing flexibility.

---

5 Equity Swaps: Bartering Shields for Spears

On the night of sack, Achaean captains donned captured Trojan armor to confuse defenders. Swapping equity achieves parallel misdirection—trading asset skins so each party protects what the other lacks.

Common version: an owner contributes real property into an operating partnership—often an UPREIT via Section 721 exchange—in return for operating-partnership units. They defer capital gains, diversify risk, and tap professional management.

You, the sponsor, inject a stabilized trophy into your portfolio with minimal cash expenditure, issuing units at negotiated valuation.

Key mechanics:

- **Contribution Agreement** detailing working-capital adjustments, environmental warranties.

- **OP Unit Conversion Schedule** controlling when old owners can redeem into REIT shares, preventing dilution waves.

- **Put/Call Windows**—call protects you if redevelopment is strategic; put protects them if liquidity cramps.

On smaller scale, equity swaps appear as tenants-in-common trade ins: a partner relinquishes interest in Deal A for equalized interest in Deal B plus boot. Either way, paper morphs into paper, cash stays holstered, and tax arrows glance off shield rims.

---

6   Additional Horse Designs

While our headline tactics dominate mid-market playbooks, creativity spawns variants:

- **Preferred-Equity Waterfalls** where investor receives priority coupon then converts to participating common at stabilize—mirrors hidden troops emerging later.

- **Convertible Seller Notes** flipping into JV equity upon refinance, sharing upside for deferring rate.

- **Reverse Contracts for Deed** letting buyer assume risk and reward while title lags, ideal where lender defeasance prepayment is punitive.

- **Pledge of LLC Interests** enabling off-record transfers past stringent due-on-sale clauses.

- **Wraparound Assumables** layering new consideration atop a vintage three-percent HUD loan—troops concealed behind a forty-year amortization ramp.

The pattern is constant: study barrier, embed solution inside a form the other party welcomes.

---

7   Due-Diligence Sleights and Ethical Lines

Odysseus' ruse skirted divine law; the poet excuses or condemns depending on the singer. Investors must honor modern law lest the horse backfire.

Non-negotiable ethics:

1. **Full Disclosure to Counter-Parties and Lenders.** Concealing side letters voids insurance, invites felony charges.

2. **Compliance with SAFE-Act and Dodd-Frank** when
   crafting seller-carry in owner-occupied or consumer
   contexts.

3. **Fair-Housing Guardrails** when executing lease-options;
   option consideration cannot become disguised
   discriminatory barrier.

4. **Tax Counsel Opinion Letters** on equity swaps to forestall
   IRS re-characterization.

Within these lines, creative structuring is celebrated ingenuity;
outside them, it's wooden treason.

---

8   The Cost of Misreading the Oracles

Recall Laocoön, priest of Apollo, who warned:

> "O my countrymen, what madness! Do you think
> the foe is gone? Or any gift from Greeks
> comes without guile? Either this timber hides
> Achaean steel, or bolts to scour our walls…"

Had Trojans heeded, history pivots. Likewise, bankers and
appraisers read structures with suspicion. Misaligned incentives
invite loan committee spears.

Common stumbling points:

- **Over-levered Combined Loan-to-Cost** when seller carry pushes total debt beyond policy.

- **Appraisal Shortfall** where wraparound artificially inflates resale value.

- **Cash Flow Thinness** after preferred returns subtract; DSCR fails covenants.

- **Future Dilution Fears** from convertible notes triggering unknown cap tables.

Mitigation: present the paradigm openly, provide scenario tests, and underwrite to worst-case—no troops springing after close.

---

9   Case Study: The Steel-Milled Victory

A Midwest sponsor coveted a 1960s, rail-served warehouse contiguous to his existing logistics park. Seller demanded ten million; appraisers landed at 8.5. Bank would lend six. Sponsor proposed:

- Two-million cash.

- Four-million senior loan.

- Two-million seller note at four percent, interest-only five years, then amortize ten.

- Two-million equity units granting seller fifteen-percent promote after eight-percent preferred.

Seller deferred tax, kept income, and believed in park upside. Bank blessed structure: LTV 47 percent, DSCR 1.45. Within thirty months, sponsor rezoned surplus land to outdoor storage, boosted NOI thirty-three percent, refinanced, paid note, and everyone hailed the scheme. Creative finance turned appraisal gap into joint windfall.

---

10 Case Study: The Horse That Burned

A hospitality group pursued a beachfront hotel with hurricane damage. They inked a master lease with option to buy, assumed insurance claim rights, and pledged to rebuild rooms. Option strike sat above realistic post-rebuild value; still they forecast IRR twenty-five percent. Year two, NFIP tightened payouts, and state building codes demanded pier elevation. Construction costs doubled. Lease payments drained reserves. Sellers kept option fee and retook an asset partly gutted. Lesson: a horse built without accurate cost intelligence delivers disaster to its makers, not its target.

---

11 The Deal-Structure Brainstorm Template

Creative structures flourish when teams suspend hierarchy and court unlikely angles. Use this script in a two-hour workshop—whiteboard, coffee, roles rotated.

Phase One – Barrier Name

Start with the wall. Examples: *price too high*, *seller tax pain*, *cap-ex uncertainty*, *rate volatility*, *title seasoning*, *low appraised value*.

Phase Two – Opponent Incentives

List what the other side craves: steady income, clean exit, legacy, speed, discretion, control, prestige.

Phase Three – Available Materials

Inventory your resources: private note investors, option funds, 1031 pipeline, assumable loans, expertise insiders, municipal grants.

Phase Four – Concealed Mechanics

Combine items into Trojan prototypes:

- Lease-option with shared upside on rezone.

- Seller note convertible to OP units.

- Wraparound using existing HUD note.

- Preferred equity fronting renovation draw with look-back IRR triggers.

Phase Five – Risk Punch-List

For each design, answer:

- Does lender permit?

- Does tax law bless?

- Worst-case cash burden?

- Public perception blow-back?

Flag red lights; refine until amber or green.

Phase Six – Story Draft
 Craft a one-paragraph narrative pitched from seller or lender perspective. If it reads like a gift horse they naturally desire, you have echo of Odysseus' poetry. If it sounds convoluted, redesign.

Conclude meeting by assigning diligence action items and outside-counsel opinion triggers.

---

12   Scaling the Art: Training Junior Strategists

Veterans smell structuring gaps; newcomers mimic surface forms. Teach mindset, not memorized playbooks.

- **Shadow Negotiations**—junior staff attend closings, observe personality chess.

- **Deal Post-Mortems**—break down failed proposals; ask, "Where was the spear hidden?"

- **Legal Draft Labs**—mock redline sessions with corporate counsel on clause language.

- **Incentive Alignment Exercises**—role-play as seller to surface emotional leverage.

Within a year, analysts begin spotting carry-back talk tracks or option frameworks without prompt.

---

13   Moral Boundaries: When Cunning Becomes Betrayal

Odysseus weeps in later poems for soldiers who died by his trick. Investors cross a line when they camouflage risk so thoroughly the counter-party cannot evaluate consent.

Guardrails:

1. **Plain-English Summaries** cover each complex clause.

2. **Mutual Counsel Encouragement** ensures other side retains representation.

3. **Transparency on Exit Assumptions**—don't bury aggressive cap-rate compression.

4. **Commitment to Post-Close Relationship**—remain available for clarifications.

Commerce rooted in honor travels farther and costs less in litigation.

---

14   Creative Financing amid Rising Rates and Tight Credit

Just as Zeus sent stubborn winds to confound homeward Greeks, central banks can tighten liquidity. That environment amplifies Trojan-style advantages:

- Seller notes bridge higher leverage caps.

- Lease-options bypass immediate take-out debt exposure.

- Convertible equity tempts family offices yearning yield without asset management.

- Assuming vintage HUD/Fannie notes with sub-three-percent coupons creates instant arbitrage.

Expect regulators to eye non-traditional leverage; document at institution-grade standard.

---

15 Final Chorus: Carrying the Horse

"And they hauled the horse up to the citadel
with ropes and songs, and blind with joy threw wide
the looming gates that none could breach by force."

Your objective is the same: inspire counterparties to invite your structure in willingly. They must sing as they pull. Behind planks and paint wait disciplined spreadsheets, rock-solid covenants, and a vision crisp enough to survive inspection.

Outsmart, do not outmuscle. Let sold-out syndicators raise ever larger battering rams while your team rolls timber on greased skids—quiet, precise, inevitable. At dawn, when lenders and rivals wake, they will find the standard of your investors flying from the parapet, the keep secured, and your creativity legendary.

Draw your brainstorm template. Name the walls. Carve the horse. Night is falling; the guards grow drowsy with wine. Time to wheel imagination against stone.

Chapter 8 — Hector's Wall (Asset Management)

1   The Prince Who Held the Line

Every midnight torch along the Trojan battlements knew Hector's shadow. He was the hinge on which the city's survival swung—commander, morale officer, repairman in armor. Unlike Paris, who drifted between chambers and prayer cushions, Hector paced the parapets, checking stone courses for cracks, reforging spearheads, rotating fresher troops to weak gates. Homer sketches the routine in crisp strokes:

> "And Hector ranged the ranks with watchful eyes,
> heart steady as a shield unseen but felt,
> bidding each man brace timbers, set fresh stakes,
> for walls unfought decay to ruin."

Nothing glamorous clung to patching ramparts, yet every hour spent adjusting buttresses postponed the Greeks' breach. Defense, Hector knew, was not a heroic pose but a non-stop discipline of upkeep.

Modern asset managers confront less lethal sieges: leaking roofs, rent escalations, HVAC rebellions, zoning inspections, tenant unrest. The empire they defend is Net Operating Income. Their wall is occupancy. The moment attention drifts, vacancy arrows fly.

The lesson translates neatly: preservation of cash flow is a pulse to be taken daily, not a policy filed once.

---

2 Tenant Retention: Guarding the Gate

A resident deciding whether to renew is Achilles testing the wall for cracks. Stop them at the gate, you keep the city; lose them, and the enemy camps on your lawn. Tenant retention is cost-effective defense: renewing a lease costs roughly one-third of sourcing a new occupant once concessions, marketing, and downtime add up. Yet many landlords chase fresh signings like Trojan nobles chasing glory sorties and ignore the rank-and-file within.

Rituals of Retention

1. **Quarterly Pulse Calls.** Every lease anniversary minus ninety days, on-site staff phones residents, asks three questions: How's the living experience? How's maintenance response? Any feature could improve life here? Record answers; assign tickets inside twenty-four hours.

2. **Rolling Upgrade Credits.** Instead of waiting for turnover to install new pulls or LED fixtures, offer residents upgrade menus they can trigger for modest rent bumps. Each completed upgrade is a fresh length of timber added to the wall.

3. **Tenant Story Database.** Trojan elders knew each soldier's clan; property managers must note birthdays, pet names, job wins. Push a congratulatory card; loyalty cements.

4. **Defensive Communication Windows.** Hector spoke at dawn and dusk when fear spikes. Managers send monthly newsletters on the first workday and fifteen days before rent due—two touchpoints hedging rumor mills about remodels or ownership change.

Retention is not grand strategy; it's vigilant friendship. As Hector told his brother:

> "We guard their sleep because our own depends on it."

So do renewals.

---

3   Cap-Ex Timing: Stones in the Mortar

Standing on the rampart, Hector directs masons to wedge fresh slabs the day hairline fractures appear, not when daylight pours through. Capital expenditures follow the same principle: intervene early, position budgets cyclically, avoid emergency premiums.

Sequencing Guidelines

- **Five-Year Reserve Scan.** Plot roofs, boilers, pavement, paint on a rolling sixty-month horizon. Assign month and budget range. Share with investors so no one feigns surprise when scaffolds appear.

- **Seasonal Cost Arbitrage.** Replace chillers in October when HVAC contractors bid lean; paint exteriors in shoulder seasons when crews discount to fill calendars.

- **Stacking Projects to Minimize Vacancy.** Pair window replacements with interior turns so the same vacancy serves multiple upgrades.

- **Funding Strategy.** If refinance proceeds or supplemental debt fund a large capital wave, spend highest energy-savings items first—LED retrofits, insulation—so lowered utilities immediately ease DSCR stress.

Delay is expensive. Trojans who skipped overnight buttress checks found ladders hooked at dawn. An asset manager who postpones asphalt crack-seal will repave entire lots next spring.

---

4 Preventive Maintenance: The Night Patrol

Hector's sentries stamped cold feet on ramp stones and scanned for loose pickets. Preventive maintenance echoes that patrol—small cycles, repeated. The objective is invisibility; catastrophe prevented never writes a headline.

Core Cycle

- **Weekly Walk-Throughs.** Property manager and maintenance lead circle exterior, note gutter clogs, leaning fences, cracked caulk.

- **Monthly Mechanical Logs.** Record boiler pressures, chiller temps, elevator ride counts; trend deviations trigger work orders.

- **Quarterly Roof & Attic Review.** Drone or ladder, you choose. Punctures sealed before rains find gypsum.

- **Semi-Annual Safety Audits.** Inspect extinguishers, emergency lighting, GFCI outlets; test alarms; document for insurance.

- **Annual Vendor Tune-Ups.** HVAC, plumbing, fire suppression—service contracts stipulate date ranges; tie vendor pay to completion reports.

Preventive discipline converts spiking expense curves into low plateau lines. In war verse: arrows are cheaper than spears; fix drains before you rebuild ceilings.

5   The 12-Month Ops Calendar: March-to-March Siege Rhythm

To weld retention, cap-ex, and prevention into one drumbeat, craft a living calendar. Begin in whichever month you close the asset; for simplicity we'll march January to December, but your pattern slides.

January — Kick-off budget meeting; distribute reserve schedule; negotiate bulk supply contracts.

February — Lease-renewal blitz for spring expirations; market survey of comparable rents and concessions.

March — HVAC preseason tune-ups; spring landscaping prep; launch resident community event (coffee cart, fence-painting volunteer day).

April — Roof walk post-winter; crack-seal asphalt; send Q1 investor letter with KPI dashboard.

May — Pool compliance checks; student-housing turn plan if applicable; order exterior paint bids.

June — Execute paint or siding projects; commence peak leasing push; evaluate insurance renewal quotes.

July — Mid-year budget revise; reserve transfers; host tenant appreciation BBQ; deploy smart-lock pilot in one building.

August — Boiler inspections; fall marketing collateral; set holiday cap-ex cutoff.

September — Pavement line-striping; lease-option analysis for upcoming expirations; fire system annual certification.

October — Chiller shutdown; heater start-up; gather winterization materials; send lender compliance packet.

November — Begin preventative snow plan; finalize next-year capital allocations; early-bird renewals for January leases.

December — Audit vendor W-9s; finalize insurance; host holiday gathering; write annual investor narrative ("the war report").

This wheel never stops; at December's dusk, January's budget sunrise gleams. A manager who obeys the wheel replicates Hector's midnight watch: continuous, calm, exact.

---

6 Metrics as Arrow-Slits: Seeing the Field

Walls without arrow-slits blind defenders. Metrics reopen vision.

- **Economic Occupancy** (rents actually collected ÷ gross potential) warns of hidden breaches.

- **Work-Order Completion Time** tracks handyman agility; above forty-eight hours signals staffing cracks.

- **Cap-Ex Variance** compares actual spend against calendar; deviations > 10 % require command huddle.

- **Renewal Spread** (new rent vs prior) indicates pricing power; negative spreads mean enemy ladders rising.

- **Preventive Compliance Score** (tasks completed ÷ tasks scheduled) floats like a banner; strive for ninety-five percent.

Publish dashboards monthly. Transparency is the drum that keeps defenders in tempo.

7 Case Study: The Wall That Quietly Crumbled

A coastal owner acquired a 160-unit complex, boasted ninety-eight percent occupancy. They delayed roof replacements to juice early-year cash yield. Hurricane season came; wind peeled shingles; water infiltrated fireplaces. Insurance fought coverage over worn condition. Three building pods vacated for mold remediation. Occupancy plunged to eighty-five, DSCR crashed; lender sniffed default. Total damage cost triple the saved reserves. Lesson: cap-ex deferred is breach invited.

8 Case Study: The Garrison That Held

An inner-ring suburb asset manager followed the full calendar. They rotated three buildings for proactive plumbing re-pipe before leaks appeared, swapped fluorescents to LEDs, installed parcel lockers requested in last year's tenant surveys. Renewal offers came with amenity photos, rents bumped eight percent while submarket averaged four. Maintenance backlog fell to two days. When a city inspector arrived unannounced, every extinguisher tag was current. Investor letter nicknamed the staff "Modern Trojans." No armies breached.

9 Behavioral Glue: Culture of Daily Stone-Setting

Discipline lives in people, not software.

- **Morning Stand-Up.** Five-minute huddle: yesterday's wins, today's tasks, one resident delight story.

- **Gamified Maintenance.** Each on-time service ticket earns shield icons; top tech monthly claims gift card. Fun sparks vigilance.

- **Whole-Team Cap-Ex Tours.** Walk jobsites; let leasing agents see pipe guts; they appreciate budgets and sell upgrades to prospects.

- **Storytelling.** Management recites "Hector moments" during all-hands—times a small act prevented a major expense. Narrative becomes culture.

Homer's Hector embodies responsibility; make every team member steward of one brick.

---

10 Aligning Investor Expectations: Peace Between City and Treasury

Some LPs rail like restless foot soldiers if distributions dip during preventive cycles. Counter tension with foresight:

- **Lifecycle Graphs** in offering memoranda show reserves and cap-ex peaks.

- **Quarterly Photologs** portray ongoing works—visual proof of future value.

- **Milestone-Based Distribution Triggers** tie extra dividends to occupancy and expense benchmarks, aligning patience.

Investors, like Trojans, endure hardship better when leaders narrate purpose.

---

11 Technology as Reinforced Stone

Sensors, software, drones—these are iron clamps across Hector's wall.

- **IoT Water Leak Sensors** alert phones before drywall stains.

- **AI Lease Pricing** auto-adjusts offers to meet renewals ahead of competitor concessions.

- **Drone Roof Scans** produce centimeter mapping; data stores in preventive module.

- **Maintenance Apps** route tickets, store appliance serials, schedule filter replacements by algorithm.

Tech is not glamour for pitch decks; it's mortar resisting time.

---

12   Final Guard at Dusk

Hector knew his life would end beneath Achilles' spear, yet he carried on:

> "I have learned to stand in courage always,
> to fight among the foremost ranks of Troy."

Asset management shares that resolve. Storms, markets, aging infrastructures—some spear will pierce eventually. But the measure of stewardship is how long and how profitably you hold the line before that day.

Plot the calendar. Patrol the halls. Replace the tiles before they fracture. Speak with tenants as fellow citizens behind one wall. Do these things each dawn, and like the resilient city Homer mourns yet admires, your property will outlast sieges, pay tribute to investors, and earn epics in the mundane ledgers where wealth endures.

Chapter 9 — The Gods Intervene (Regulatory Shifts)

1   "Zeus Turned the Tide": When Lightning Strikes Strategy

In the *Iliad* nothing breaks a battle line like a god's impulse. One moment Hector drives the Greeks to their ships; the next, Poseidon surges from the surf and rallies the Achaeans. Plans crumble, courage flickers, and commanders scramble to read a sky alive with omens.

> "Then Hera touched the cloud amassed on Ida's peak,
> and Zeus, seeing, bent his dark brows; suddenly
> the whole plain boomed beneath a crashing bolt,
> and men who thought they knew the day's design
> found chaos underfoot."

No mortal in Homer's world can out-duel such force. They can only anticipate, build reserves, and pivot when thunder rolls. Real-estate investors live in a similar cosmos. Zoning boards, tax writers, central bankers—deities of modern finance—hurl amendments and rate hikes that rewrite underwriting in an hour. Yesterday's safe harbor turns to shallow reef; yesterday's marginal lot becomes gold. Survival lies in the same skill Achilles practiced before he charged: watch the sky, polish the bronze, and be ready to change footing at the first flash.

2   Mapping the Pantheon of Policy

- **Zoning Commissions** are Athena, goddess of civic order—sometimes gifting density bonuses, sometimes defending single-family sanctums with spear and glare.

- **Congress and Parliament** resemble Hera: jealous, political, able to bless or curse whole fleets with a clause tucked on page 980 of a budget bill.

- **Central Banks** are unmistakably Zeus, hurling voltage down the yield curve. A twenty-five-basis-point thunderbolt can vaporize value assumptions overnight.

- **State Tax Authorities** mirror Apollonian archers: their arrows—credits, abatements, new depreciation schedules—strike from far, silently changing holding-period math.

- **Environmental Agencies** occupy the Poseidon role, bringing tidal waves of compliance: wetlands setbacks, gas-ban edicts, storm-water mandates.

- **Courts** stand in for Themis, goddess of law, settling landlord–tenant disputes with gavel swings that reshape cash flow for entire metro areas.

Understanding who may act is the first defense; understanding when they act is the second; and hedging how they may act is the art that keeps sails intact when the gust arrives.

---

3 Zoning Metamorphosis: From Siege Ramp to Secret Gate

3.1 The Lightning of Up-Zoning

A strip of tired warehouses hugs a commuter rail line. One Tuesday evening, the planning commission votes to rezone the corridor for eight-story mixed-use. By dawn, land that traded at twelve dollars per buildable square foot is worth thirty-five. Owners who heard rumors have term sheets ready; those who slept wake to bidding wars they cannot enter.

Counter-example: a suburban council, under ballot pressure, down-shifts the maximum Floor Area Ratio for multifamily on parcels near schools. Projects penciled at 2.0 FAR suddenly strangle at 1.2. Equity scatters. Lenders invoke force-majeure walk-away clauses. The sponsor spends eighteen months lobbying for variances that never arrive.

3.2 Watching Athena's Loom

Hector posted lookouts on every tower; investors post watchers on every agenda.

- **Calendar Patrols.** Subscribe to city-clerk feeds, commission live streams, and neighborhood-council notifications. A junior analyst should scan agendas weekly, flag items with keywords—"density," "overlay," "historic," "inclusionary."

- **Relationship Quadrants.** Break bread early with planning staffers, traffic engineers, and economic-development officers. When a draft ordinance circulates, allies ping you before PDFs hit public drives.

- **Scenario Coding.** For each target parcel, map three future-zoning paths—restrict, status quo, expand. Model coverage ratios, height limits, parking counts. Keep underwriting toggles ready; when news drops, you reload assumptions in minutes, not weeks.

Athena's favor feels arbitrary only to the uninformed. Those who study her weave of hearings, memos, and pilot programs see the pattern and move before thread tightens.

---

4 Tax-Law Tweaks: Apollo's Arrows on the Balance Sheet

4.1 Depreciation Shifts—Sunrise or Sundown?

In 2017 the U.S. Congress expanded bonus depreciation to one hundred percent for certain property components. Sponsors who grasped cost-segregation science mined millions in first-year deductions, slashing taxable distributions and supercharging after-tax yield. But bonus depreciation phases down; each sunset year recasts cash-on-cash returns. Deals birthed in sixty-percent bonus climates must survive at forty, twenty, and zero.

Europe echoes the tension: when the United Kingdom introduced the Structures and Buildings Allowance, London funds pivoted to long-life assets; when France toyed with wealth-tax surcharges, French institutional REITs re-weighted cross-border.

4.2   Credit Regime Reboots—Energy, Low Income, Historic

Congress, like Hera, loves to dangle favor then yank. Solar-investment tax credits extend, expire, re-extend. Low-Income Housing Tax Credits adjust volume caps, attract capital or starve it. State historic programs lapse when budgets tighten. Sponsors relying on these arrows for capital stacks must track legislative calendars as closely as they track vacancy reports.

Tools to dodge Apollo's shifting light:

- **Tax-Policy Radar Groups**—join industry coalitions that lobby and circulate draft bills before public release.

- **Phase-Out Laddering**—front-load projects qualifying for sunsetting incentives; push later phases into more stable depreciation buckets.

- **Exit-Scenario Tax Models**—calculate disposal gains under both current and proposed codes; pre-negotiate 1031 accommodation or 721 contributions if step-up rules shift.

Apollo's ray can fertilize crops or parch them; rotation and irrigation—timing and structure—decide which.

---

5 Interest-Rate Shocks: Zeus Drops the Hammer

5.1 Thunder on the Yield Curve

March 2022: the Federal Reserve lifts rates for the first time in three years. By December short-term benchmarks rocket four hundred basis points. Bridge loans closing at LIBOR+250 reset near seven percent. Multifamily cap rates lag, valuations squeeze, sale volume plunges. Sponsors heavy on floating debt scramble for rate caps; premiums spike tenfold.

Zeus does not warn. Investors must assume storm cycles.

5.2 Rate-Risk Tool Kit

- **Rate Caps as Standard Gear.** Never model floating debt without a purchased cap; treat premium like property insurance—embedded.

- **Forward-Starting Swaps and Treasury Locks** when permanent financing sits nine months out.

- **Debt-Service Resilience Bands.** Stress every pro-forma five hundred basis points. If DSCR dies at +150, you court lightning.

- **Bridge-to-Fixed Ladders.** Stage rehab draws so you can rate-lock segments upon completion, slicing interest-rate exposure into tranches.

- **Reserve for Cap Premium Renewal.** When caps expire mid-hold, set aside incremental reserves yearly.

Hector could not bribe Zeus, but he could thicken the wall; sponsors cannot bribe the Fed, but they can armor the balance sheet.

---

6 The Macro-Risk Radar: Cockpit for Storm Pilots

6.1 Four Screens, One Glance

Screen One — Legislative Tracker. Bills by status, sponsor, committee; colored ribbons: red for tax, blue for zoning, green for environmental. Updates weekly.

Screen Two — Economic Thermals. Fed fund futures, 2/10 yield-curve slope, CPI prints. Auto-alerts when rate-hike probability crosses fifty percent.

Screen Three — Regulatory Sentiment. Scraped quotes from key commissioners, mayors, finance ministers. Tone-analysis algorithm tags hawkish, dovish, pro-development, anti-landlord.

Screen Four — Project Exposure Map. Heat map of portfolio weighted by debt type, incentive reliance, zoning variance dependency.

A dashboard condenses divine whispers into visible vectors.

6.2   Data Feeds and Rituals

- **Monday Ritual.** Analyst summarizes weekend political news, new bills, central-bank speeches. Slides in ten minutes of the ops call.

- **Quarterly War Room.** Executive team pressure-tests portfolios against worst-case policy combos: rent control + rate hike + tax sunset.

- **Annual Oracle Summit.** Invite lobbyists, municipal planners, ex-Fed economists. Half-day Q&A, live document edits to macro-risk playbook.

Ritual matters. Greeks burned thigh bones to read smoke; you burn hours reading spreadsheets. Both create foresight.

---

7   Case Study: The Rezoning Coup

A small syndicator owned two acres of suburban retail boxes. County announced a transit-oriented-development overlay. Because the syndicator's radar flagged public-comment sessions months earlier, he hired a traffic consultant, prepared renderings, and lobbied. When ordinance passed, his land leapt from 0.3 FAR to 4.0; he joint-ventured with a mid-rise apartment builder, rolled equity tax-deferred, and multiplied basis by eight. Rivals on adjacent parcels, unaware, sold cheap at "retail exit" valuations.

---

8   Case Study: The Rent-Cap Snare

An institutional buyer closed on a two-thousand-unit Sun Belt portfolio under floating debt at seventy-five percent LTC, March 2023. Six months later the state legislature enacted emergency rent caps—five percent plus CPI. With operating expenses surging nine percent, underwriting collapsed. Lender triggered cash-sweep, mezz partner seized GP position. The buyer's risk radar ignored state-house rumblings flagged by industry associations; lightning struck invisible.

---

9   Building Organizational Reflexes: From Panic to Pivot

9.1   Liquidity Barracks

Hold at least six months fixed operating expenses and debt service in revolvers. Zeus rarely gives nine-month notice.

9.2   Legal Contingent Plans

- Draft pre-clearance for condo-conversion docs if rent caps bite.

- Maintain fallback land-bank partnership agreements in case of zoning downshift—sell air rights, retain fee simple.

- Keep at-the-ready property-tax-protest packages; appraisal district swings after up-zoning can double assessments.

9.3   Communication Drill

When gods speak, rumors race. Prepare template letters to tenants and investors explaining policy impacts, outlining timelines, promising updates. Silence breeds panic; clarity calms.

> "Better to know the storm at once," Odysseus counseled his oarsmen, "than fear each gust unseen."

---

10   Ethics of Influence: Playing in Olympus Without Hubris

Lobbying is legal; bribery is Troy horse gift reversed. Build credibility, not secret passages.

- **Transparent Donations** within caps; disclose to stakeholders.

- **Public Comment** with data not threats.

- **Coalition Building** with housing advocates when goals align—mixed-income overlays, green-space credits.

- **Respect Democratic Outcome.** If the city votes renter protections, pivot strategy rather than sue reflexively; win hearts before courts.

Hubris enraged gods; humility partnered them.

---

11 The Long View: Accepting Divine Cycles

Markets over centuries outlast any single statute. Achilles accepted fate; investors accept cycles. Regulatory frost may linger years; then fresh councils thaw. Hedged reserves and opportunistic land banking position you to strike when rules flip.

Homer ends not with policy solved but with Priam begging for his son's body—politics, grief, and mercy entwined. Real-estate stories never close; they roll from zoning board to refinance to inheritance. The task is not to dominate gods but to steward capital through their moods.

---

12 Action Summary—Forge Your Macro-Risk Radar

1. **Identify Deity Equivalents**—map each property's exposure to zoning boards, legislatures, tax codes, interest

rates, environmental agencies.

2. **Set Data Pipelines**—agendas, bill trackers, economic feeds, sentiment scrapers.

3. **Assign Watch Officers**—analyst for agendas, controller for tax, CFO for rate risk.

4. **Stress-Test Quarterly**—model revenue under three regulatory shock combos; schedule mitigations.

5. **Maintain Liquidity and Hedge Arsenals**—FRAs, caps, swaption pockets, standby letters of credit.

6. **Engage Early**—join chamber boards, neighborhood councils, policy roundtables; shape drafts, don't merely react.

7. **Educate Stakeholders**—publish digest, hold war-rooms, share thunder forecasts.

8. **Refine Continuously**—after every shock, debrief radar accuracy and adjust sensors.

Closing Invocation

"Sing, Muse, of the fickle gods who tilt the fates of men;

teach us to read the sky, to guard our camps,
to store dry powder in the cave before rain."

Keep the radar glowing. When the next ordinance gavel cracks or the Fed chair clears his throat, your team will already be shifting shields, tightening jest, and redistributing weight for the new vector. Strategy endures not by resisting heaven but by bending sails to its winds—an art as old as Homer and as urgent as tomorrow's committee vote.

Chapter 10 — Patroclus in Borrowed Armor (Partnerships & Joint Ventures)

---

1 "He Buckled on the Greaves": What the Episode Means

Achilles sulks beside his beached ships, wounded in pride. His friend Patroclus, anguished by the slaughter of Greeks, begs to borrow the famous armor and rally the Myrmidons. Achilles relents:

> "Put on my glorious armor, lead my men,
> and drive the Trojans back—only ward off ruin;
> do not pursue the lord of horses, Hector."

Patroclus accepts the commission, but once the clangor of battle fills his ears, he forgets the limit. Inflamed with borrowed prestige, he chases the Trojans to their gates and falls beneath Hector's spear. Homer shows the double-edged nature of substitution: armor multiplies power yet masks vulnerability; stepping into another's mantle can carry one past the boundaries of mandate and competence.

---

2   The Modern Parallel: GP–LP Dynamics and JV Roles

In real-estate finance the "armor" is control—the right to originate, approve draws, sign debt, hire vendors, call capital. The GP (general partner, managing member, sponsor) normally wears it. Limited partners supply bulk equity but sit behind protective clauses; they influence through covenants, not command. Trouble brews when either side tries the borrowed-armor maneuver:

- **LP Mission Creep.** A big check entices an investor to demand day-to-day vetoes, turning a silent equity seat into de facto management—without tested skill or local knowledge.

- **GP Over-Delegation.** A sponsor, stretched thin, hands substantive duties to a co-GP who flashes brand but lacks underwriting rigor. Revenue misses and deadlines expose gaps the emblematic title concealed.

- **JV Identity Confusion.** Two developers merge for scale—one excels at ground-up entitlement, the other at stabilized operations—yet neither codifies decision lines. Meetings devolve into turf wars; lenders hear the strain and price risk accordingly.

Partnership is not bad; misaligned partnership is lethal. Patroclus proves that intention and friendship do not override structural limits. Achilles discovers too late that armor without spirit cannot guarantee outcome.

3   The Spectrum of Partnership Layers

Think of partnership as concentric circles of authority:

1. **Vision Setting.** Define asset class, geography, risk profile.

2. **Capital Formation.** Source debt, equity, incentives.

3. **Execution Control.** Secure entitlements, manage construction, oversee leases.

4. **Reporting & Governance.** Produce financials, adhere to covenants, conduct audits.

5. **Exit Decision.** Choose refinance, sale, or hold beyond term.

Every party wears some plate across each circle. GP usually dominates rings three and five; LP buys weight in rings two and four; vision may be co-crafted. If any circle is understaffed, a hole opens. If two people tug one piece of bronze at once, seams split.

4 Patroclus Syndrome: Markers and Outcomes

4.1 Flashy Co-GPs

A celebrity sponsor appears, promising capital firepower, demands half promote, but dispatches junior staff to underwriting calls. Red flags:

- Missed deliverables.

- Reliance on high-level slide decks over rent-roll analysis.

- Lender questions answered with non-numbers.

Armor borrowed: brand equity. Risk: lender rejects loan, delaying rear equity draw, burning earnest money.

4.2 Dominant LPs in Disguise

Family office writes 85 percent of equity, asks for independent-right voting rights "on material decisions," then widens definition to include vendor selection, staffing, even temperature setpoints. GP becomes asset manager by name only, morale sinks, turnover rises, project stalls.

Armor borrowed: control. Risk: paralysis, staff attrition, LP self-dealing allegations.

4.3   Silent-But-Deadly Local Partners

Out-of-state fund teams with local developer who promises municipal relationships. JV grants local minority GP slice but majority control of entitlement process. Emails unanswered; hearings slip. Outsider steps in, but chain of command and indemnities confuse officials; permit clock resets.

Armor borrowed: credibility. Risk: timeline drift, budget overruns, blame spiral.

---

5   True Strength: Matching Metal to Muscle

Patroclus was skilled but not Achilles. The correct lesson is not to refuse partnership, but to size the armor to the wearer.

- **Capability Alignment.** Map each role to documented track record—permits won, units stabilized, exit IRRs realized.

- **Capital Alignment.** Weight promote distribution to risk actually borne. A guarantor who signs carve-out carries dose of danger LP capital does not.

- **Decision Protocol.** Hard-code thresholds: cap-ex change orders above X dollars require dual signatories; leasing below Y per square foot triggers consultation; refinance substitute debt must meet DSCR and LTC bands.

- **Sunset & Removal Clauses.** If performance flakes, armor reverts. For GP removal: cause definitions tie to misapplication of funds, fraud, willful breach, or key-man loss with cure windows.

The central question before granting armor is: Who suffers if misuse occurs? Paper answers must survive litigation heat.

---

6   Incentives: Pulse Beats Under Bronze

Armor is neutral; incentives animate. Homer hints: Patroclus enters the melee to preserve comrades, but the lure of glory corrupts focus. Partnerships must engineer reward systems that keep combatants inside mission lanes.

- **Performance Fees vs Asset Fees.** Acquisition fees upfront can seduce GP to volume over diligence. Shift weight to promote on realized value add.

- **Preferred Returns with Catch-Up.** LP sees downside cover; GP retains upside, discouraging early cash-out demands.

- **Hurdle Staircases.** 8/10/12 percent IRR hurdles escalate promote shares; both parties push for efficiency.

- **Claw-Backs.** Promote claw-back after final liquidation controls premature victory laps.

A term sheet outlining incentives is the rivet connecting
co-commanders to shared destiny.

---

7   The Partnership Term-Sheet Checklist

Before signatures, walk through each bullet as if a spear might
slide between gaps:

1. **Parties and Percentages.** Legal names, state of
    formation, capital contributions, ownership interests.

2. **Purpose and Scope.** Single asset or programmatic?
    Development or acquisition? Geographic boundary?

3. **Capital Commitment Schedule.** Initial equity, future draw
    mechanics, capital-call notice periods, default remedies.

4. **Debt Strategy.** Target leverage, guarantor obligations,
    carve-out allocations, approval standard for refinancing.

5. **Governance.** Managing member powers, voting
    thresholds, major decisions list, deadlock resolution
    (buy-sell, mediation).

6. **Distribution Waterfall.** Return of capital, preferred return
    rate, catch-up percentage, promote splits, claw-back test
    frequency.

7. **Fees.** Acquisition, asset management, construction,
    disposition, refinance, guarantor, development—amounts

or formulas, payers, timing.

8. **Reporting & Audit.** GAAP or tax basis, quarterly packages, annual audit requirement, LP inspection rights, confidentiality.

9. **Key-Man and Staffing.** Named individuals, substitution rights, grace period, removal triggers, non-compete edges.

10. **Transfer Restrictions.** Lock-up period, ROFR, tag-along, drag-along, pledge of interests guidelines.

11. **Removal & Replacement.** For-cause definitions, notice, cure, interim manager, promote forfeiture mechanics.

12. **Exit.** Minimum hold period, sale approval metrics, listing authority, listing broker veto rights, rights to buy internal interests before open market.

13. **Indemnities & Insurance.** GL, D&O, builder's-risk, who is additional insured, cap on indemnity.

14. **Tax Matters.** Partnership representative appointment, 704(c) allocations, depreciation method, withholding obligations.

15. **Dispute Forum & Governing Law.** State, arbitration vs court, venue, attorney-fee clauses.

Tick every item; attach exhibits for budgets, pro-formas, management agreements. Patroclus died unarmored at the throat; a term sheet is your gorget.

---

8   Case Study: The Fragile Borrowed Mantle

A boutique multifamily sponsor partnered with a Middle-East sovereign fund. The fund required veto power on vendor selection above $50,000. Six months in, local GC bids arrived $200,000 higher than predicted. Sovereign insisted on offshore contractor network. City licensing blocked foreigners; project froze. Carry costs ate pref return, IRR cratered from 18 percent to 9. Post-mortem: veto was armor mis-sized; sponsor should have capped procurement veto at national firms pre-vetted with jurisdiction.

---

9   Case Study: Right-Sized Collective Victory

Conversely, a senior-housing operator joined forces with a regional hospital chain. Operator retained property management; hospital provided land and patient flow. Term sheet clear:

- Hospital veto limited to clinical programming, not paint colors.

- Operator promote scaled with resident satisfaction metrics.

- Annual cap-ex funded 60/40; hospital's share convertible into rent reductions for qualifiers.

Project reached 92 percent occupancy year two, above-market margins, quick refinance. Armor fit; roles aligned.

---

10 Communication—The Liner under the Plate

Bronze chafes flesh; linen padding matters. Weekly steering calls, monthly KPI decks, quarterly site walks cultivate trust. Include:

- Unit-level P&L, occupied vs economic occupancy, delinquency roll.

- Schedule of cap-ex versus budget.

- Market comps and marketing spend.

- Debt-compliance certificate snapshot.

- Risk dashboard—litigation, code compliance, insurance claims.

Silence fosters suspicion, suspicion breeds intervention, intervention cracks helm.

---

11   Succession and Continuity

Achilles was irreplaceable; when he withdrew, chaos ensued. A JV must script leadership contingency:

- Second-in-command list with authority tiers.

- Digital vault for passwords, loan docs, emergency contacts.

- Board or advisory committee ready to vote interim manager.

Investors buy durability, not charisma.

---

12   The Emotional Undercurrent: Pride, Trust, Fear

Patroclus sought honor equal to Achilles'. Partners bring ambitions. Acknowledge motives in kickoff retreat—money, prestige, community impact. State openly how the waterfall serves each desire. Where motives clash, redesign splits; forced altruism breaks late.

> "Yet I, too, longed to shine among the foremost,
> and glory called me onward past the bounds you set,"
> Patroclus whispers as life ebbs.

Do not let unspoken glory quests guide boardroom swords.

13 Exit Psychology

When Trojan battlements finally fall, spoils ignite new quarrels. Exits trigger greed, tax panic, legacy questions. Pre-wire:

- Drag-along triggers after set year and IRR floor.

- Forced-sale rights if buyout offers exceed appraisal by spread.

- Put/call if hold period hits double business plan.

Model after-tax yields for each partner type; share scenarios. Exits shock less when rehearsed.

14 Regulation Overlay

Securities laws treat co-GP solicitations as capital formation; obtain placement-agent licenses or rely on Reg D safe harbors. ERISA investors require plan-asset mitigations, independent fiduciary. FIRPTA hits foreign units. As armor smith tests every rivet, compliance counsel stress-tests term sheet lines.

15 Final Reflection

"He fell, and the armour rang upon him,
    fair, shining, new, and now stained with dust."

Patroclus' tragedy underscores that armor is more than metal; it is identity, responsibility, covenant. Partnerships and joint ventures stand or topple on clarity of role, proportionate incentives, and mechanisms to return borrowed plate before zeal outraces competence.

Draft the checklist. Walk each clause aloud. Look every partner in the eye and ask: *Will you stay within your lane when battle cries swell?* Secure a yes in signed ink. Only then shoulder shields, align spears, and march.

Chapter 11 — The Skirmish Over the Ships (Liquidity Crunch)

I. Flames on the Beach: The Moment Supply Lines Snap

The turning point of the *Iliad* is not Achilles' feud or Hector's last stand but a brief, blistering fight at the water's edge. Greek ships—their only road home and the only conduit for grain, bronze, wine, and reinforcements—lie beached in neat rows. When Hector breaks the front and hurls torches toward the hulls, every king understands that if those vessels burn, the war ends in famine and slaughter. Homer's camera tightens:

> "Hector seized a blazing brand,
> and the flame leapt high as he cried aloud:
> 'Now, fire, devour the swift ships—
> let smoke darken the sky and choke their hope of
> flight!'"

In minutes, years of provisioning may vanish. An army that weeks earlier boasted heroes now trembles at the thought of empty bread sacks and no retreat path. Liquidity—literal and logistical—has reached zero.

Transposed to modern portfolios, the ships are cash balances and credit facilities. They ferry payroll, interest coupons, capital-ex draws, emergency roof repairs, and tenant-improvement allowances. Burn them—run dry or lose banking partners—and the campaign ends no matter how promising the spreadsheet once looked. The lesson is stark: protect the supply line or forfeit the war.

II. Understanding Liquidity: The Three Arteries

1. **Cash Reserves** – immediate, unrestricted funds sitting in operating and cap-ex accounts.

2. **Committed Credit** – revolving lines, construction revolvers, bridge facilities, corporate credit cards.

3. **Capital Markets Exit** – the refinance or sale that converts illiquid equity into replenished coffers.

If any artery clots, pressure drops across the organism. Investors often obsess over the third—exit IRR—while ignoring the first two. Homer reminds us the first failure usually occurs behind the front lines: a cookhouse out of flour, a carpenter without pitch, a treasurer without cash.

III. Early Warning Signs of a Ship-Side Skirmish

- **Vendor Payables Stretching Past Net-45.**
  Like foot soldiers missing rations, contractors begin hinting at work slow-downs.

- **Operating Account Drains Below One Month of Fixed Charges.**
  Repairs get triaged; morale on site drops; occupancy falters.

- **Rate Caps Approaching Expiry Without Replacement Quotes Funded.**
  Akin to storm clouds over the fleet with no tarpaulin ready.

- **Refi Term Sheets Slip From Q2 to "Later in the Year."**
  Decision makers postpone because DSCR projections no longer clear lender hurdles.

- **Unexpected Draw Holds by Construction Lenders.**
  Inspectors cite slow progress, freeze disbursements pending new equity.

Each signal echoes the Trojan cry on the sand. Wait until torches touch planking and rescue costs triple.

IV. Building the Buffer: How Much Cash Is Enough?

There is no commandment carved on Olympus; instead, craft ratios grounded in local reality.

- **Operating Reserve Rule.** Keep a minimum of three months of fixed expenses (principal, interest, insurance, taxes, payroll, and contracted services) accessible within 48 hours.

- **Cap-Ex Reserve Rule.** Hold 10 percent of remaining budget in an overnight-ready account even when lender reimburses expenses; disbursement delays are certain in crunch moments.

- **Cushion for Variable-Rate Exposure.** If any debt floats, warehouse at least three months of worst-case incremental interest (calculate at current index plus 200 bps above stress cut).

- **Unencumbered Cash Percentage.** At the GP or corporate level, maintain at least 5 percent of portfolio gross revenue in unrestricted cash—usable to cure covenant breaches or support capital calls.

These formulas are shields stacked edge-to-edge; each slows burn velocity.

V. The Role of Revolvers and Corporate Lines

Cash alone can't lift a fully loaded trireme off the sand; you need draft from deeper water—committed credit that expands quickly, costs little when idle, and closes before smoke thickens.

- **Size to Two Quarters of Operating Deficit at 25 percent Vacancy.**
  Stress test worst-case: what if half your tenants stop paying for three months? Size the revolver so you can float until courts or subsidy catch up.

- **Maintain Clean-Down Covenant.**
  Agree to zero balance for 30 days each year; forces fiscal discipline, reassures banks you are not using the line as permanent leverage.

- **Cross-Collateral Consideration.**
  Limit cross-default to ring-fenced asset groups; when one property falters you don't drag the fleet.

- **Auto-Renew Trigger.**
  Build renewal option six months ahead of maturity; Zeus loves last-minute storms—remove that calendar peril.

Failure to secure credit early resembles Greeks waiting to forge spears until the Trojans crest the trench.

VI. Refinancing: The Retreat Route

Even if cash burns and lines tap out, a successful refinance or sale can ferry survivors. But exits require liquidity in lenders' coffers—and yours.

Timelines
 Begin refinance diligence 12 months before maturity, even in benign markets. If recession threats loom, 18. Hector reached the ships in an afternoon; capital markets can freeze within a quarter.

Equity Stack Readiness
 Have a contingency pledge from existing LPs or sponsor capital equal to at least 10 percent of current principal in case appraisal comes short.

Hedge Forward
 Where fixed-rate coupons are attractive, lock at application. Where spreads feel wide, pay 30 day extensions—not 90—preserving optionality.

Broker Rotation
 Engage two brokerage teams: one primary, one shadow. Should first lose focus amid pipeline glut, the second can take the file without orientation lag.

Odysseus held a reserve crew aboard hidden ships; mimic his paranoia.

VII. The Burn-Rate Calculator: A Sword Instead of a Guess

Fear recedes when math enters. The calculator lives on one sheet and answers in minutes:

- **Input**

  - Gross Potential Rent

  - Current Economic Occupancy

  - Fixed Expenses (taxes, insurance, payroll, utilities, debt service)

  - Variable Expenses (% of revenue)

  - Cap-Ex Outflows (by month)

  - Available Cash Reserves

  - Committed Revolver Capacity

  - Cap Stack Cushion (unfunded LP commitments, sponsor capital)

- **Output**

  - Monthly Net Cash Flow Under Three Scenarios: base, minus 10 % revenue, minus 25 %.

- Months Until Exhaustion of Reserves.

- Date Revolver Hits Limit.

- DSCR Breach Projection Date.

- Equity Call Requirement to Maintain Solvency.

- Earliest Safe Refinance Window Given Debt-Yield Targets.

Open weekly. Homer's heroes sharpened blades each dawn; asset managers refresh burn-rate charts.

VIII. Case Study: The DVB Bridge Gone Dry

A sponsor purchased an eighty-five-unit urban rehab with a Deutsche Pfandbrief bridge at SOFR + 350, two-year term, one-year extension, no rate cap mandated. Pandemic shutdowns slowed permits; carry lengthened six months. Interest expense climbed as SOFR doubled. GC liens froze more draws. Burn-rate sheet showed reserves empty in 45 days. Sponsor pulled a 750k revolver only to discover the bank invoked Material Adverse Change and reduced capacity. They pivoted to mezz but rates killed DSCR. Asset sold at break-even. Lesson: ships without layered supply lines sink.

IX. Case Study: The Self-Storage Rampart That Held

A small operator in the Southeast modeled burn at 50 percent vacancy (hurricane risk). They raised extra sponsor capital upfront, bought a two-year rate cap, and secured a $1M revolver with no clean-down clause. Year two, storms toppled power lines; property shut for six weeks. Insurance delays and revenue dip drained 40 percent of cash, but revolver plus cap payout kept DSCR above lender triggers. Refinance closed six months later on schedule. Investors received 17 percent IRR. Supply lines preserved victory.

X. Behavioral Dynamics: Panic Versus Protocol

When torches flare, humans sprint or freeze. Liquidity management absorbs emotion into pre-written moves.

- **First Alarm Rules.** If reserves drop below two months of fixed costs, controller must notify executive committee within 24 hours; committee meets within 72.

- **Spend Hierarchy.** Payroll, insurance, debt service, life-safety repairs—paid in that order. Cosmetic upgrades pause automatically.

- **Capital Call Playbook.** Drafted during fundraising, including mechanism, notice period, default interest, dilution formula. Borrowers will sign when skies are blue.

- **External Communication.** Lender receives early warning; better to signal struggle than surprise. LPs get narrative plus action plan; panic muted by transparency.

We emulate Nestor's calm exhortation:

> "My friends, the ships are stout, the sea is wide;
> but hold your ground, obey the cry,
> and every man may yet see dawn."

Protocols steady hearts.

XI. The Role of Insurance in Liquidity

Property, flood, business-interruption, builder's-risk: each sends dollars when disaster clicks the stopwatch. Yet filings lag.

- **Policy Structure.** Business-income coverage period must match realistic rebuild timeline; 12 months is seldom enough for major structural loss.

- **Advance Payments Clause.** Negotiate carrier advances within 30 days of initial proof. Without, reserves must bridge entire adjuster cycle.

- **Blanket Versus Scheduled.** Blanket allows flexibility if one building fries but another stands; scheduled limits cannot reallocate easily.

Carriers are reluctant bankers; still, treat them as secondary supply ships.

XII. Portfolio-Level Diversification of Cashflow Timing

Stagger lease expirations, interest resets, and maturity dates so cash inflows offset drains. Hector flung all torches at once; diversified calendars dilute impact.

- **Ladder Debt** across quarters, not one maturity month.

- **Allocate Cap-Ex Waves** by region to spread contractor draws.

- **Cross-Train Staff** so overtime at one asset equals saved temp hires elsewhere.

Synchronization thrills but sinks fleets; weave asynchronous safety nets.

XIII. Shadow Banking Threats: The Trojan Torches You Don't See

In boom cycles sponsors lean on debt funds and CLO loans. When capital-market tide ebbs:

- Funds impose discretionary holdbacks.

- Warehouse lenders demand mark-to-market re-margin calls.

- CLO liquidity triggers accelerate amortization.

Arguments citing term sheets fail; only standby cash cures.

XIV. Government and Regulatory Siege Engines

- **Tax Reassessments.** A sudden jump in valuation can erase reserve forecasts. Protest aggress-ively but pre-fund probable escrow hikes.

- **Rent-Moratorium Edicts.** Courts stall evictions; occupancy appears but cash-in flows shrink. Revolver should anticipate such freeze scenarios.

- **Environmental Compliance Deadlines.** Gas-ban retrofits drain capital budgets; plan phased rollouts matched to cheap financing windows.

As gods meddle, so may city councils.

XV. The Human Factor: Sponsor Reputation as Invisible Reserve

Vendors and lenders extend grace to leaders known for honesty and quick payment in good times. Cultivate that goodwill; it becomes a short-term line of credit when flames crackle. Conversely, a history of nickel-and-diming erodes slack.

> "Even Troy's foes honored Hector's word,"
> the poet reminds; reputation can buy hours enough to douse sparks.

XVI. Implementing the Burn-Rate Calculator Across the Team

1. **Template Standardization.** One format for all assets; populate via data pulls from property-management software.

2. **Cloud Version Control.** Live link prevents outdated files.

3. **Dashboard Integration.** Feed outputs to red-amber-green visual on exec home screen.

4. **Quarterly Audit.** CFO reviews formulas; errors slip in as budget spreads evolve.

5. **Training.** Every assistant property manager learns to run the sheet; knowledge redundancy mirrors multiple water buckets.

XVII. Future-Proofing: Preparing for the Next Torch

- **Sustain 18-Month Rolling Liquidity Plan** updated monthly.

- **Pre-Clear Alternate Lenders** with full due-diligence data room ready for emergency sends.

- **Maintain War Chest Vehicle**—a separate LLC funded by management fees that can swing into deals as mezz or preferred equity at market rates.

- **Insurance Renewal Shopping** 120 days out; early bids arm you to force incumbent concessions freeing cash.

- **Continuous Improvement Loop**—after each liquidity scare, hold a post-mortem, amend reserve policies, raise next fund with lessons inscribed.

XVIII. Closing Exhortation

The night Hector reached the prows, Ajax the Greater planted himself astride the gangway and roared:

> "Friends, be men; reserve in your hearts
> the shame that generations will speak
> if fire consumes the ships that brought us here!"

Ajax's bulk mattered, but the unbroken line of shields behind him saved the day. In the arena of finance, shields are dollars, credit covenants, exit timelines, and the vigilance of burn-rate math. Stand them edge to edge before the first spark. Nurture reserves, renew lines, rehearse exits, and lift the calculator every Monday. Then, when torches arc through dark air, you will answer not with panic but with sober buckets ready—supply lines intact, campaign alive.

Chapter 12 — Achilles Returns (Aggressive Repositioning)

1   Smoke, Grief, and the Moment to Strike

For nine books Achilles idles in righteous fury, brooding while comrades bleed. Then Hector kills Patroclus. Achilles rises from the sand, drenched in grief and sudden purpose, and vows to re-enter the fight. Homer marks the shift like a seismic crack:

> "So saying, he donned the flame-bright mail,
> and the great helmet tossed its horsehair plume
> so terribly, it seemed a star born at noon."

The tide turns in hours. Greeks who had rationed arrows brace shields again; Trojans who sang of victory taste dust. Timing is everything: Achilles' surge lands precisely when the enemy's confidence peaks and the defending line sags. The lesson for investors is clear. A property can languish under mediocre rents and fading paint for years, yet a well-timed capital assault—money, design, and marketing fused—reverses fortune with shocking speed. Repositioning is not a tweak; it is Achilles bolting across the trench, sudden and overwhelming.

2 The Anatomy of a Surge in Commercial Real Estate

Repositioning is bigger than deferred maintenance and smaller than ground-up construction. It is a mid-campaign maneuver designed to convert an aging or misaligned asset into the highest and best use that current demographics, technology, and culture will reward. The three engines match Achilles' triple weapons—spear, shield, chariot.

1. **Capital Injection (The Spear).** Fresh equity or opportunistic debt buys drywall, boilers, balconies, fiber, art, foliage, training, and time. Without that thrust, nothing pierces market complacency.

2. **Heavy Value-Add (The Shield).** Physical work—gut renovations, amenity builds, energy overhauls—defends against future obsolescence the way Achilles' iron shield repels Hector's volley.

3. **Re-Branding (The Chariot).** Once walls gleam and systems hum, the story must change: new name, new colorway, new digital persona, new leasing scripts. A chariot's speed translates effort into momentum.

If any piece is missing the surge slows. Pumping money into cap-ex without a brand reset is like Achilles fighting in borrowed armor—powerful but anonymous. Rebranding without fixes is parade paint on rotten planks. Capital without timing risks overpaying for improvements just before a macro downturn.

3   Sensing the Inflection Point

Achilles did not sprint cold. He waited until Trojan spears licked fire at the ships. The inflection point in property life shows similar smoke:

- Occupancy skids despite market rent growth—tenants perceive tired product.

- A peer asset completes renovation and captures eight-percent rent premium.

- Deferred maintenance list tops ten percent of annual gross revenue.

- Local employers pivot to hybrid work, freeing daytime parking for adaptive reuse.

- Interest rates dip enough that cost of capital undercuts anticipated rent lift.

When two or more flare, battle horns call for surge. Delay and you fight uphill against eroding cash flow and higher construction costs.

4   Funding the Return—Capital Injections That Hit Hard

Bridge-to-Bridge Recapitalization.
 Replace maturing bridge debt with new, larger bridge proceeds. Lender underwrites post-renovation value; sponsor draws difference into cap-ex escrow. Risk: rising rates compress exit, but advantage is speed—the spear is already in hand.

Preferred-Equity Shock Troops.
 A mezzanine or pref layer drops above common equity, pays fixed coupon until refi. The coupon looks like Achilles' unstoppable stride: expensive, blunt, decisive. Works when senior lender balks at LTC but cash-on-cash after lift dwarfs pref coupon.

GP Capital Over-Contribution.
 Sometimes the sponsor must bleed. Injecting personal funds at zero coupon signals conviction; LPs rally behind like Myrmidons hearing Achilles promise vengeance. Guardrail: document step-in promote for the over-fund.

Government and ESG Grants.
 Energy-efficiency or historic-tax credits mimic Hephaestus' shield—sophisticated, rare, protective. They lower effective equity, but paperwork drags. Only deploy if timing still favors first-mover advantage.

5 Designing Heavy Value-Add—From Tents to Tower

A superficial makeover cannot scatter Trojans; only dramatic, visibly different hardware commands rent. Core layers:

1. **Systems First.** HVAC, plumbing stacks, electrical service. Residents don't tour boiler rooms, but leaks cancel five-star Google reviews faster than dated flooring.

2. **Structural Modernization.** Open bay warehousing to last-mile micro-fulfillment; garden apartments into smart-lock, parcel-locker, pet-washing paradises.

3. **Amenity Arms Race.** Coworking lounges, pickleball courts, rooftop greens. Select two that dominate local comps rather than six diluted offerings.

4. **Unit Interiors.** Quartz and stainless still rent, but lighting design, USB-C outlets, and digital thermostats convert "lookers" to "applicants" in minutes.

5. **Curb Appeal Command.** Reskin façade, re-stripe lots, bury overhead wires, flood entry with uplighting. Achilles' plume shook like wildfire; first impression matters.

Schedule work in stacked blocks—plumbing stage, sheetrock stage—so crews cycle, not scatter. Use model-unit leasing to pre-sell rents while hammers echo.

6 Re-Branding—Writing a New Song for an Old Stronghold

No one would mistake Achilles for any other warrior once light struck his crest. Properties need equally unmistakable identity.

- **Rename.** Shed dated moniker (Sunset Arms) for magnetic concept (Forge Flats, Oxygen Lofts).

- **Visual Language.** Palette pulls from local context but sharpens saturation—charcoal and copper rather than beige and brown.

- **Narrative Hook.** Target demographic story: "Built for remote creatives," "Rooted in craft-beer culture," "Mindful living near trailheads." Authentic beats aspirational fluff.

- **Digital Siege Engines.** Drone tours, influencer collaborations, social proof loops. If photos aren't shareable, surge fizzles.

- **Staff Re-Forge.** Leasing agents rehearse new script, uniforms echo palette, maintenance uses branded vans; every point of contact reaffirms metamorphosis.

Remember: re-branding fails if legacy reputation lingers. Achilles circled camp in new armor; he did not hide rage behind a scarf.

7 Sequencing the Attack—When to Strike

Achilles re-enters only after Patroclus falls but before ships ignite—a razor window. Repositioning performs best when:

- **Interest-Rate Windows.** Capital cheaper than historical average but trending upward—borrow ahead of competition.

- **Supply Pause.** New construction pipeline slows due to permits or cost spikes; upgraded asset leaps in quality while new deliveries stall.

- **Demographic Wave.** University expansion, hospital build, or corporate relocation announced; value-add times with occupancy spike.

- **Policy Incentive Sunset Nears.** Start renovation early to beat code revisions; like Achilles sprinting before night falls.

Surge too early and capital sits idle waiting for tenants to catch on; too late and rent premiums already priced.

---

8 The Reposition Feasibility Grid—Turning Vision Into Numbers

Instead of a table, envision a five-lane roadway you must clear:

Lane One: Physical Feasibility
Walk every unit, pop ceiling tiles, snake cameras down drains. If structure cracks past cost to repair, detour.

Lane Two: Financial Feasibility
Model new rents using verified comp leases, subtract realistic concessions, and stress interest 150 bps over forward curve. If year-three DSCR stays below 1.20, emergency shoulders may vanish.

Lane Three: Market Feasibility
Interview brokers, employers, civic planners. Ask not "What are asking rents?" but "Which amenities closed leads last quarter?" If area wages can't justify premium, surge meets shield wall.

Lane Four: Operational Feasibility
Can current management execute bigger budget? Bring third-party specialists early; Achilles without Myrmidons is celebrity without chorus.

Lane Five: Exit Feasibility
Identify at least two buyer profiles or lenders who crave finished product—core funds, DST sponsors, life companies. Document their yield boxes. If no buyer type deems cap rate plausible, glory fades.

Clear all lanes; burn-rate sheet becomes war map.

---

9 Risk Edges and Mitigations

- **Construction Inflation Spikes.** Lock labor contracts, buy long-lead materials up front, hold five-percent contingency.

- **Lease-Up Drag.** Pre-lease at discount tiers, escalate after 50-percent occupancy, keep marketing spend flexible.

- **Interest-Rate Lift Mid-Project.** Cap or swap; hold right to convert bridge to perm once stabilization crosses ninety-day threshold.

- **Brand Misfire.** Pilot-test colorways and amenities on social focus groups before painting every balcony purple.

- **Sponsor Bandwidth.** Hire dedicated reposition director; weekly war rooms maintain tempo.

---

10 Case Study: The Mill District Miracle

A forty-year-old brick warehouse in a second-tier city floated at sixty-eight-percent occupancy. Sponsor raised five million in pref equity, layered twelve-million bridge, poured six million into seismic retrofit, skylights, coworking loft, and rooftop deck. Re-named Steel & Grain. Within fourteen months rents jumped thirty-two percent, NOI doubled, cap-rate compression added eight million of value. Timing: city announced tech-hub tax zone just as renovations began; competitor new builds stalled in permitting.

11   Case Study: The Too-Late Loft

Another sponsor waited until two luxury towers opened across the street before starting heavy value-add on an aging mid-rise. Debt high, construction costs peak, brand message "retro luxe" muddled. Lease-up at new rents lagged; refinance appraisals depressed. Surge mistimed; Achilles arrived when Trojans had regrouped.

12   Leadership Psychology—Fire in the Chest, Ice in the Veins

Achilles channels fury but fights with precision. Reposition command teams need emotional fuel—vision of shiny lobby, pride in environmental scores—but cold scheduling discipline. Weekly Gantt reviews, daily Slack updates, transparent KPI dashboards keep zeal tethered.

> "So Achilles moved among the ranks,
> his eyes like white flame, yet every word a measured cut—
> strike here, hold there, advance when I call."

Adopt his paradox: burning intent, surgical action.

13   Exit Strategy—Sheathing the Sword

The best surge ends before over-improvement erodes ROI.

- **Refinance** once stabilized NOI trails pro-forma by less than five percent for ninety days; cash-out repays pref and revolver.

- **Strategic Sale** into 1031 or REIT appetite while property glistens and comps still lag.

- **Hold With Dividend** if cap-rates widen; harvest cash flow until next rate valley.

Pre-write decision tree. Hesitating after victory invites counter-attack.

---

14   Long-Term Legacy—From Rage to Stewardship

When Achilles finally kills Hector, he must learn restraint or become monster. Likewise, after reposition success, governance matters: replenish reserves, refresh amenities on three-year cadence, maintain brand authenticity. Aggression yields; stewardship sustains.

---

15 Closing Invocation

> "Rise now, great Achilles, break the fear that grips the host;
> let bronze flash like dawn upon the plain."

Translate that call to your portfolio. When market smoke signals inflection and your burn-rate sheet confirms fire-power, stride. Inject capital, swing sledgehammers, paint new banners, and let prospects gasp at first tour. A well-timed surge rewrites destiny, wins rents, and earns epics in lender boardrooms. But remember the vision grid, temper fury with feasibility, and leave the field not smoldering but reborn—proof that timing, courage, and craft can bend even the oldest wall.

The ships are safe, the enemy retreats, the sun glints off fresh-forged stone. Your investors sing; the rehired tenants cheer. The surge has turned the tide.

Chapter 13 — The Fall of Hector (Cutting Losses)

1   A Spear in the Dust: The Tragic Wisdom of Retreat

On the second afternoon after Achilles' return, the Trojan prince charges once more onto the plain. The poet pauses the fight to underline what is at stake: "Hector, breaker of horses, stood fast, yet in his mind he weighed two courses." Should he call the gates shut and regroup, or hold the line in single combat? Pride wins; he stays. Achilles' spear, driven by rage and perfect timing, finds the slit in Hector's helm:

> "Bronze clanged on bone, and the point burst through;
> dark night wrapped his sight as life slid away."

With Hector's death the outcome of the war is sealed. Troy's last, best defender falls because he could not read the pivot between stubborn valor and strategic withdrawal. Homer offers a brutal footnote: knowing when to detach can save the city, the army, and the years invested. The same reality shadows every real-estate portfolio. An asset once heroic—prime corner retail, flagship campus apartments—may weaken under new competition or macro shock. Victory lies not in dying on that hill but in exiting clean, redeploying capital, and mounting a fresh campaign.

2   The Economics of Staying Too Long

Holding an underperformer drains three reservoirs:

- **Opportunity Cost** — Equity locked in a 5 percent cash-on-cash asset cannot chase the 12 percent value-add across town.

- **Management Bandwidth** — Staff hours pour into delinquent collections, lender waivers, vendor disputes, eroding attention to thriving properties.

- **Reputational Gravity** — LPs watching quarterly write-downs doubt sponsor judgment, hamstringing future raises.

A bleeding property behaves like Hector's corpse tethered to Achilles' chariot: it circles the camp, sowing horror. Better to ransom the body—sell at discount, accept bruises—and free momentum.

---

3   Signals of Imminent Collapse

Hector faced three omens: Achilles' approach, Zeus' scales tipping against him, and the panic of allies. Investors observe analogous portents.

1. **Negative Leverage Spread** — Cap rate slides below interest rate for two consecutive quarters despite

attempted rent pushes.

2. **Chronic Concession Cycle** — You raise face rents but free months balloon, revealing weak demand.

3. **Capital-Exhausted Asset** — Required cap-ex to stay competitive consumes more than thirty percent of NOI each year.

4. **Strategic Drift** — Property no longer fits buy-box defined in the charter; management expertise misaligned.

5. **Market Narrative Shift** — Municipality adopts rent caps, or a bypass reroutes traffic away from retail frontage.

When two emerge, convene war council; at three, prepare retreat.

---

4   Psychology of Holding: The Hector Trap

Why do sponsors cling?

- **Sunk-Cost Fallacy.** We have poured two million into remodel; another hundred thousand might "fix it."

- **Prestige Attachment.** Trophy asset strokes ego; selling feels like public admission of failure.

- **Loss-Aversion Math.** Paper losses hurt less than realized; sponsors gamble on time magically repairing fundamentals.

- **Confirmation Bias.** Only upbeat market reports get airtime in Monday meetings.

Hector, too, rehearses self-soothing: "Better to face him; maybe I will win immortal fame." The antidote is disciplined decision trees.

---

5 Mechanics of Exit: Selling the Underperformer

Open-Market Sale
List with a brokerage team that regularly transacts distressed or value-add inventory. Price realistically; disclose warts. Speed outranks last-dollar gain.

Off-Market Direct Play
Target buyers with complementary synergies—neighboring owner seeking assemblage, fund specializing in fixers. Conversation-driven deals close faster, with fewer retrades.

Note Sale or Assumption Transfer
If lender cooperates, assign debt to buyer; protects coverage ratio hurdles, widens buyer pool. Offload carve-out guarantees if possible.

Short Sale or Deed in Lieu
In deep impairment, negotiate graceful exit; preserves GP

reputation. Provide lender with dataroom, third-party valuation, weekly updates—professionalism buys leniency.

Achilles drags Hector round and round; you do not have that luxury. Close within the quarter.

---

6   The 1031 Exchange as Redemption Arc

Greek myth grants Hector no resurrection, but the tax code offers investors a reincarnation device: Section 1031. Selling one asset "relinquished property," rolling proceeds into a "replacement property," defers federal capital gains, retains equity mass, and keeps war chest intact.

Key commandments:

- **Identify within 45 Days** — Name three targets or the 200-percent rule list. Prepare before closing; sluggish scouts lose the window.

- **Close within 180 Days** — Align lender underwriting on day one; choose markets you already understand.

- **Match or Exceed Debt and Value** — Replacement must carry equal or higher purchase price and mortgage amount compared to relinquished. Arrange bridge equity early if valuations mismatch.

- **Beware Boot** — Cash received or debt reduction triggers taxes; track numbers to the penny.

A deft 1031 converts defeat into momentum, like Achilles forging new armor from Patroclus' shattered gear.

---

7   Strategic Upgrade: Trading Up the Risk Curve

Sometimes you do not abandon risk—you refine it. Sell stale B-class suburban offices, move into medical office anchored by hospital leases. Shift aging class-C apartments into self-storage near migration corridors. Each swap pivots exposure toward sectors where your operational shield is stronger, harvest cycles longer, and headline threats lighter.

---

8   Hold/Sell Decision Tree — Narrative Walk-Through

Root Question: Is the asset on track to achieve or exceed pro-forma returns within stated timeline?
- **Yes** –> *Hold*, monitor quarterly.
- **No** –> Proceed to next branch.

Branch Two: Can a realistic, budgeted reposition push NOI above break-even DSCR inside 18 months?

• **Yes** –> Evaluate capital stack; if reserves or cheap credit available, reposition surge.
  • **No** –> Proceed to next branch.

Branch Three: Does asset serve a strategic or regulatory hedge (tax credit, zoning bank) valuable to portfolio?
  • **Yes** –> Consider joint venture buy-in; dilute but keep advantage.
  • **No** –> Proceed to exit branch.

Exit Branch: Model sale scenarios—open market, off-market, note sale, short sale. Select path with highest risk-adjusted return after tax. Begin 1031 search day of LOI acceptance.

Implement internal decision cutoffs: once asset reaches Exit Branch the order is binding; no back-pedal unless new data emerges. Discipline saves lives.

---

9 Debt and Covenant Considerations in Retreat

Lenders are battlefield allies or jailors. Pre-flight checklist:

- **Prepayment Penalties** — Yield-maintenance or defeasance can wipe seller proceeds; negotiate fee-waiver in exchange for early warning.

- **Debt-Yield Caps** — Some lenders restrict sale below specified price unless loan defeased; plan cash cover.

- **Springing Cash Management** — Triggered by DSCR shortfalls; cure or negotiate release upon contract signed.

- **Assumption Fees and Underwriting** — Prep buyer packages to streamline approval.

Proactive communication mirrors Priam approaching Achilles with ransom—humble, open-handed, detailed. Zeus favors candor in negotiations.

---

10   LP Relations: How to Tell the Story of Loss

Investors fear incompetence more than red ink. Quarterly letters must:

1. **Own the Numbers** — Present variance versus underwriting.

2. **Explain Drivers** — Macro shift, competitive supply, mis-executed lease-up.

3. **Show Options Matrix** — Hold with further spend, JV pivot, sale pathways.

4. **Recommend Course** — Summarily back decision tree outcome.

5. **Project Capital Distribution** — Net of taxes, debt retirement, fees.

Invite Q&A calls, publish minutes. Transparency transforms grief into renewed confidence, ensuring LPs fund next campaign.

---

11   Cultural Discipline: Building a Retreat-Friendly Organization

Tacticians drill "break contact" maneuvers as vigorously as frontal assault. Portfolio managers should:

- **Schedule Annual Hold/Sell Workshops.** Each asset advocates for its keep, dragon-den style.

- **Establish Objective Scorecards.** Weighted metrics: NOI trend, cap-ex drag, market elasticity, strategic fit.

- **Reward Early Warnings.** Bonus staff who flag failing KPIs early; do not shoot messengers.

- **Document Post-Mortems.** After sale, archive lessons—overoptimistic rent pushes, underestimated regulatory friction.

A team fluent in strategic withdrawals sustains longer wars.

---

12   Case Study: The Mid-Rise Mercy Kill

A 1990s downtown office building once thrived at 96 percent occupancy. Pandemic remote work slashed physical tenant demand to 55 percent; two anchor leases due in nine months signaled non-renewal. Upgrade to life-science labs cost $400/ft—impossible. Sponsor triggered decision tree: no feasible reposition, little strategic value, debt yield below threshold. Listed quickly; a charter school network purchased at educational-use valuation. Sponsor executed 1031 into grocery-anchored retail in growth suburb. IRR hit only 6 percent versus 14 percent pro-forma, but saved capital from further decay and captured bonus depreciation on new asset.

---

13   Case Study: The Riverside Redemption

Class-B garden apartments on riverfront flooded twice in three years. Insurance premiums soared; NOI cratered. Before selling at zombie price, sponsor discovered a city greenway initiative paying top dollar for floodplain parcels. Off-market sale closed at a 25-percent premium to broker opinion, enabling 1031 into upland Class-B+ apartments. Loss theoretical turned into portfolio renewal—because management scouted alternatives before despair set.

---

14 Tax Strategy Beyond 1031: Opportunity Zones, 721, and Installment Sales

If timeline precludes 1031 or partners need liquidity, consider:

- **Section 721 UPREIT Contributions** — Trade asset into REIT operating partnership, defer gains, gain unit liquidity.

- **Installment Sale** — Spread gain over term, lower yearly tax bite; works when buyer confident and interest income acceptable.

- **Qualified Opportunity Fund Swap** — If asset sits in OZ but investors outside time window, sell to QOF aggregator; premium often outweighs tax friction.

Every maneuver echoes Priam's ransom ingenuity; craft options before confronting Achilles.

---

15 Guarding Against Over-Pruning

Cutting losses differs from panic dumping. Maintain core portfolio diversity, avoid selling cyclically healthy assets purely to chase fads. Decision tree prevents emotional fire-sale cascades. Ask:

- Does holding still generate uncorrelated cash flow?

- Is negative variance truly structural?

- Will sale jeopardize lender diversification tests or brand presence?

Balance is Hector's unrealized counsel: fight, but choose the field.

---

16   Final Lessons from the Corpse Beside the River

After Hector dies, Priam risks everything to retrieve his son's body. Achilles, moved, grants twelve days' truce for mourning. The war pauses, not ends. Selling a wounded asset is similar: grieve the lost upside, honor the capital spent, then march on.

> "Thus they laid Hector to rest, breaker of horses,
> and over him set the stones that mark an end—
> and a beginning for those who live."

Retreat, done wisely, fertilizes new campaigns. Your ships are intact; your army freed; the next deal waits beyond the ridge. Walk away from doomed battlements with head high, balance sheet ready, and the hard wisdom that mastery means knowing when to stop fighting.

Chapter 14 — The Sack of Troy (Exit Strategies)

1 "Fire in the Doorways, Spoil in the Halls": Why the Ending Matters

For ten unrelenting years the Greeks hauled stones, buried comrades, and shoved siege ramps toward Troy's sky-bladed towers. Yet nobody—neither Nestor with his counsel nor Achilles with his wrath—declared victory at the first breach. They waited until the city itself burned, the citadel hacked open, Hector's infant son thrown from the wall, and Priam's treasure hauled ship-side. Only then did heralds blow bronze horns and carve new boasts into captured shields: *Ilios is fallen; the long war ends here.* Homer's point is blunt: triumph is not the moment your spear pierces a gate; it is the hour you march through the ashes carrying irreversible proof that the campaign is finished. In property investing the gate is the **exit**—sale, refinance, fund wind-up, or portfolio rollover. No underwriting, rent lift, or capital injection is complete until your investors receive wired proceeds and tax forms. Victory lives in the Net-Proceeds column; all else is theater.

> "And they lit the roofs, and red gold ran like water,
> and the sea-wind fed the flames that sang of
> conquest."

An exit well timed converts sweat, debt, and risk into distributable coin; an exit bungled melts years of effort into acrid smoke. You therefore plan the sack before you launch the siege. Every hammer that nails a joist, every marketing dollar, every Friday KPI email must echo with the same unspoken question: *How does this feed the exit?*

---

2   The Four Classical Modes of Departure

2.1   The Flip—Torch and Run

In Homeric imagery, this is the sudden rush through a breach, loot in sacks, sails already rigged. Real-estate flips aim for short holds—twelve to thirty-six months—where value creation outpaces market drift. Renovate fifty kitchens, spike rents, off-load to the next risk tier. Flips thrive on speed, leverage, and recently starved buyers. Their danger: lightning-strike interest hikes and supply flood.

2.2   The Refinance—Tribute Without Leaving

Here the Greeks spare a district for ransom, siphoning wealth while maintaining a garrison. A refinance pulls cash out against new loan proceeds yet leaves ownership standing. Refi exits demand stabilized NOI, favorable rate spreads, and minimal prepayment costs. They shine when cap-rate compression flatters valuations or when fixed-rate money dips. Downside: leverage creep and balloon-maturity traps.

2.3 Portfolio Sale—The Auction of Empires

This is the wholesale liquidation of Trojan vaults—goblets, diadems, embossed armor—bundled for Mycenaean kings. Selling multiple assets in one deed package attracts institutions hungry for scale, commands tighter cap rates, and rips out headache variance. But negotiations drag, legal costs spike, and a single due-diligence snag can tank nine-figure closings.

2.4 Syndication Wind-Up—Burning the Wooden Horse

When the last plank of the deal is spent and pref waterfalls zero out, sponsors dissolve the entity, file final K-1s, scatter partners to new fleets. Wind-ups test organizational hygiene: Was every inspection recorded? Were reserves reconciled? They also crystallize promote—GP keeps a share only after LP hurdles clear. A sloppy wind-up stains reputations like smoke on bronze.

---

3 Choosing Your Siege Clock—Timing the Exit

Achilles does not sprint the instant the horse's belly unlatches; first he watches where sentries bunch, how panic rises. Likewise, the investor searches for converging signals:

- **Yield Curve Alignment**—When long-term debt costs undercut current cap rates by a full point, buyers armed with agency or life-company mortgages swarm.

- **Capital-Market Sentiment**—Track fundraising reports; dry-powder peaks mean eager allocators.

- **Asset-Specific KPI Plateaus**—Occupancy above 95 percent for three months, concessions below market average, maintenance tickets flat. Plateaus mark max stabilization.

- **Regulatory Horizons**—New rent caps or tax sunsets—exit before restraints clamp.

- **Competitive Pipeline**—Monitor upcoming supply; sell before 800 class-A units deliver down the street.

Pick the earliest shared intersection: high valuation, low tax friction, minimal future Cap-Ex, and no immediate macro thundercloud. Walk away while cheers still echo.

---

4   Designing the Spoils Caravan—Distribution Waterfalls

Homer lists the loot: tripods, horses, women "with deep waist-belts of gold." Modern waterfalls list return of capital, preferred return, catch-up, then promote. Sequence decides morale.

1. **Return of Capital**—Principal goes home first; investors stop checking midnight emails.

2. **Preferred Return Accrual**—An 8 percent-simple or IRR threshold cleansed before GP sees bonus.

3. **Catch-Up**—Sponsor may receive a segment—often 30-50 percent—to true-up parity.

4. **Promote**—The true war bounty: GP earns 20-40 percent of remaining proceeds.

Hard-code audit windows, claw-back conditions, tax hold-backs. The more transparent the chain, the fewer spears thrown across the counting table.

---

5   Tax Warfare—Shielding the Plunder

Trojans hid gold idols in temple crypts; investors shelter gains in code allowances.

- **1031 Exchanges**—Defer capital gains by reinvesting. Requires sprint—45-day ID, 180-day close.

- **721 UPREIT Merges**—Swap property for operating-partnership units, diversify, defer, gain liquidity windows.

- **Installment Sales**—Spread gain recognition; viable when you trust buyer's solvency.

- **Opportunity-Zone Redeploy**—Roll gains into QOF within 180 days, soak additional basis step-ups.

Pair each tactic with state-law overlays and depreciation recapture strategies. Flips seldom qualify; refinances dodge recognition entirely but load new risk. Weigh cost of shields versus fleet speed.

---

6   The Exit-Mapping Template—A Verbal Blueprint

a. Mission Re-statement
Define in one fierce sentence why this asset exists: e.g., *"Harvest cap-rate compression via mid-rise reposition, exit when NOI hits $2 million and cap rates hold sub-5."*

b. Trigger Metrics
Set numeric gates: occupancy, NOI, DSCR, market cap rate ceiling, required buyer yield, time left on rate cap, lending tenor.

c. Contingency Windows
For each trigger, write "If not met by X date, pivot to Strategy B (refi) or Strategy C (three-year hold)."

d. Stakeholder Notice Plan
Document who hears first: lender, equity, key vendors. Draft sample letters to pre-empt confusion.

e. Brokerage Shortlist and Scouting Orders
Name at least two brokerage teams; include criteria: historical volume, asset-class niche, buyer network. Initiate soft whispers six months before listing.

f. Legal and Accounting Prep
Catalog environmental reports, permit close-outs, lien waivers, rent roll certifications, trailing-twelve and YTD financials. Upload to data-room skeleton now.

g. Tax-Option Matrix
Pre-run 1031, 721, straight sale, refinance equity-recap models; highlight after-tax IRR under each.

h. Marketing Narrative Draft
Craft story: location drivers, value-add runway, cost-seg leftover, demographic trends. Replace bullet points with full sentences so copy is plug-and-play.

i. Timeline Gantt in Weeks
Week 0: board approval; W 2: broker RFP; W 8: OM ready; W 12: call for offers; W 16: buyer selected; W 20: PSA signed; W 36: close; W 38: distributions; W 40: K-1 drafts. Michigan cold fronts and holiday lulls flagged.

j. Post-Exit Capital Deployment Stub
Where will freed equity sail? Reallocate to new acquisitions, unit repurchases, GP dividends—state amounts and deadlines.

Commit the map to shared drive; review each quarterly ops call.

---

7   Flip Deep Dive—Blade Fast, Blade Clean

A flip exit thrives on narrative velocity. Window for highest price opens when rent surge validates underwriting but before competing flippers replicate upgrades.

- **Photo Campaign**—Professional dawn and dusk shots, drone fly-throughs, cinematic leases.

- **Proof Package**—Show first three leases at target rents, google reviews trending upward.

- **Auction-Style Bid Day**—Tight call for offers, leverage FOMO; rumors of five bidders accelerate offers.

- **Contract Hard Money Fast**—Non-refundable earnest post-diligence; buffer against sudden Fed hike.

- **Insurance-Transfer Strategy**—Assign builder's-risk to buyer or cancel instantly; no premium wastage.

Exit delays kill IRR; schedule trades like synchronized sword chorography.

---

8 Refinance Playbook—Recurring Tribute

Metrics Gate: DSCR ≥ 1.25 on trailing-three, stabilized occupancy ≥ 90 percent, management expense ratio normal.
Process Highlights:
• Rate-lock 60 days out, purchase extension options.
• Commission fresh appraisal; send contractor sign-offs.
• Hedge forward—swap or cap—as insurance.
• Day of funding, wire pay-offs, overruns, distribute excess.

Cash-out hits GP escrow; decide reinvest versus dividend before wire lands or partners bicker.

---

9 Portfolio Sale—From Plunder to Dowry

Bundle yields:

- **Scale Premium**—Institutions pay tighter cap rates for $100 million vs $10 million piecemeal.

- **Diversification Credit**—Varied geographies lower buyer risk.

- **Process Efficiency**—One data room, one PSA, one lender syndicate.

Pitfalls:

- **Weak-Link Dilution**—One underperformer drags entire price. Spin it off or brace for haircut.

- **Closing Logistics**—Multiple title states, loan defeasance, and Estoppel chasing create gridlock.

- **Tax Complexity**—Different hold periods complicate 1031; may need partial TIC drop-and-swap.

Start two years out: align fiscal calendars, unify brand, centralize leases.

---

10   Syndication Wind-Up—The Quiet Blaze

Wind-up feels bureaucratic but reputational stakes equal battlefield heroics.

Checklist:

- Finish final capital events: refi or sale.

- Clear all escrow balances—tax, insurance, replacement reserve.

- Obtain lender release letters and SNDAs.

- Distribute funds per waterfall, retain 10 percent hold-back for 90 days.

- Issue final K-1s; engage CPA early to meet March 15.

- File certificate of termination with secretary of state.

- Archive digital documents for seven years.

After wind-up, send investors debrief deck—what worked, what bombed. Transparency fertilizes next raise.

---

11 Risk Mines at the Gate

- **Environmental Surprises**—Phase I looks stale; buyer's Phase II reveals dry-cleaner plume. Order your own six months earlier.

- **Tenant Estoppel Mutiny**—Anchor retail tenant uses leverage to renegotiate. Have back-up LOI with shadow anchor.

- **Insurance Claims Pending**—Open claim lowers buyer loan; settle or escrow.

- **Title Defects**—Ancient easements surface. Clean title long before listing.

Mapping mitigations into exit plan is the difference between smooth convoy and ambush alley.

12 Human Dimension—Exit Emotions

Achilles weeps even while drenching robes in victory spoils; years of rage leave exhaustion. Exits stir nostalgia, greed, relief, and fear among partners.

Manage with:

- **Pre-Set Role Scripts**—CFO signs payoff; asset manager handles buyers; investor relations writes memos.

- **Quiet Rooms**—No last-minute strategy shifts in public Slack channels.

- **Celebration Budget**—Dinner, charity donation, or bonus pool. Closure matters.

13 Case Example: The Three-Headed Exit

A Southeastern value-add fund owned:

- A suburban 144-unit multifamily at 94 percent occupancy post-renovation.

- A 60-thousand-square-foot flex industrial with seven years of Amazon 3PL lease left.

- A class-C downtown office at 68 percent leased.

Exit map decided:

- Flip the multifamily to REIT hungry for Sun-Belt exposure—closed in four months.

- Refinance industrial asset at lower cap rate; cash-out redeployed.

- Office sold in carve-out of portfolio sale; haircut accepted to close bigger package.

Blended LP IRR hit 19 percent; GP promote cleared 3.2 million dollars. Victory declared.

---

14   The Final Torch—Why Planning Starts at LOI

You cannot stage a wooden horse in a week. You cannot craft exit terms in final month. Embed clauses in original loan docs: assumption rights, prepay caps, carve-out survivability. Draft operating agreements with drag-along rights, sale-approval thresholds. Build Cap-Ex tracking to feed appraisal. Every early brush stroke paints the last scene.

---

15   Closing Epilogue

> "And the wind caught the broad sails,
> and stern waves glittered under moonlight,
> carrying home men empty-handed of fear,
> their holds packed full with prize."

The sack of Troy is not merely destruction; it is the translation of risk into legacy. Homesick warriors became kings because they planned how to carry spoils across the wine-dark sea. Plan your exit with the same gravity. Map the gate, count the torches, time the wind. When flames roar, step through unscorched, treasure secure, and record the day as the moment your epic stopped being story and became gold in the bank.

Chapter 15 — King Priam's Ransom (Negotiation Mastery)

1   Night on the Plain: A Walk That Ends a War

Troy already smolders. Hector is dead, his body dragged around the funeral mound of Patroclus. Achilles' tent reeks of grief and unspent rage; every Greek guard knows the mood is lethal. Yet an old man in simple linen robes crosses the corpse-strewn plain, guided by Hermes and lit only by a nervous torch. King Priam, ruler of the doomed city, has slipped through enemy lines to beg for his son's remains.

Homer slows the verse:

> "He came unseen, stood by Achilles' knees,
> and clasped the hands that murdered his beloved.
> 'Remember your own father,' he whispered."

Achilles, astonished, feels tears surge—first for his absent father, then for the man kneeling, then for Patroclus. Two enemies weep together. Moments later gold lies stacked on ox-hides; Hector's body is lifted into a wagon; twelve days of truce are declared. One act of radical empathy ends an unbreakable stalemate.

Negotiation textbooks often cite tactics—anchoring, BATNA calculation, time management. Homer shows something deeper:

the single fastest way to unlock the impossible deal is to step into the other party's grief, joy, or fear so completely that mechanics become ceremony. Priam does not recite appraisals of Hector's worth; he invites Achilles to imagine his own father's sorrow. The appeal flips Achilles' internal script from vengeance to responsibility, and the deal closes in minutes.

---

2   The Psychological Pivot: From Adversaries to Co-Authors

Why does empathy work? Modern neuroscience gives Homeric wisdom a cortical map. The human "mirror-neuron" network fires when we observe another's pain as if it were our own. When Priam says, "Think of Peleus," he turns Achilles' insulated anger into shared vulnerability. The moment both parties inhabit the same emotional frame, competitive framing collapses and cooperative framing sparks.

In real-estate transactions the same pivot changes locked negotiations:

- **Sellers drowning in tax exposure** fear losing retirement.

- **Tenants resisting relocation** fear affordability cliffs.

- **Municipalities blocking zoning variances** fear political backlash.

Talk to those fears, and stone doors swing.

3 Mapping Iliadic Empathy to Deal Flow

3.1 Win-Win Closings

A seller inherited a 1970s garden complex from parents; depreciation is fully exhausted, and a taxable sale threatens a seven-figure bill. Sponsor sees only price; stalemate. Sponsor channels Priam: *"What keeps you awake about this sale?"* Seller answers taxes and legacy. Sponsor introduces structured installment note plus naming rights for community center ("Maria Villas"). Seller gains income stream and memorial; sponsor lands basis discount. Price gap dissolves.

3.2 Seller Concessions

Retail strip loses anchor tenant. Buyer needs new roof and TI allowance but offers keep clashing. Buyer stops talking dollar amounts; asks, *"How do you picture this center five years from now?"* Seller wants vibrant hub, not boarded windows. Buyer proposes retaining seller as 10 % LP with promote upside if occupancy rebounds. Empathy reframes seller from retiree to partner; concessions on price follow.

3.3 Tenant Buyouts

Value-add play demands combining two rent-controlled units into one double. Tenants distrust "renovation" promises. Sponsor schedules kitchen-table conversation: *"Tell me what a move would mean to your family."* They fear longer commute for special-needs child. Sponsor funds two-year transit pass plus broker fee, layers cash payout. Tenants agree. Project timeline spared litigation.

Empathy is not charity; it is ROI mathematics wrapped in human language.

---

4   Priam's Seven-Step Negotiation Sequence

1. **Research Private Pain.** Hermes briefs Priam on Achilles' losses. Modern analogue: gather seller motivations—tax status, family dynamics, loan maturities.

2. **Risk Personal Contact.** Priam enters enemy camp alone. You schedule face-to-face or webcam, not email ping-pong.

3. **Offer Symbolic Tribute First.** Priam carries ransom without haggling. You acknowledge the other's contribution ("Your father built this from scratch").

4. **Invoke Shared Identity.** "Remember your own father." Translate to "I also struggled with capital-gains rollover last year."

5. **Pause for Emotion.** Homer devotes thirty lines to shared weeping. Silence your slide deck; let counterpart vent.

6. **Propose Concrete Swap.** Gold for body; price for keys; relocation stipend for vacant possession.

7. **Seal with Ritual.** Achilles orders washing of Hector, shared meal. You specify closing timeline, escrow instructions, follow-up dinner.

Skipping steps one through five triggers defensive reflexes; concessions will stall.

---

5 Advanced Techniques Inspired by the Ransom Scene

5.1 Mirrored Concessions

Priam brings gold equal to Hector's weight—a literal mirroring. In a win-win close, mirror concessions: price reduction mirrors due-diligence waiver; earlier earnest money mirrors closing flexibility.

5.2 Frame Switching

Priam reframes Achilles from enemy to son. Negotiator might reframe landlord as *community steward*, not *rent harvester*, by emphasizing facade upgrades that raise neighborhood pride.

5.3   The "Third-Story" Narrative

Ury's method: describe story both sides could tell a neutral
observer. Priam does this implicitly—two fathers mourning. Write
LOI preamble describing joint legacy: "This project preserves
mid-century masonry while providing 60 modern units."
Counterpart sees dignity, not surrender.

---

6   Constructing the Concession Trade-Sheet

A trade-sheet lists variables you can give, variables you need, and
relative valuations for both sides. Think of it as weighing gold on
Hector's scale before entering the tent.

Column A — Your Variables

- Purchase price

- Closing date

- Hard-money timeline

- Cap-Ex escrow size

- Leaseback period

- Seller note interest

Column B — Counterparty Variables

- Tax structure (installment/1031)

- Earn-out triggers

- Naming rights

- Legacy staff retention

- Environmental indemnities

Column C — Subjective Value Score
Rate 1-5 for you, guess 1-5 for them.

Column D — Possible Trades
 e.g., You raise price 2 % (cost: medium) in exchange for 90-day seller financing at 3 % (value: high).

Update in real time during negotiations; visualize win-win bundles: two low-cost-to-you, high-value-to-them concessions for one high-value-to-you ask.

---

7   Case Study: Warehouse Peace Treaty

Riverfront distribution warehouse worth $18 M. Seller retiring, demands 60-day close, no re-trades. Buyer values full nine-month diligence due to soil doubts. Stalemate.

Trade-Sheet Output:
Seller values certainty; buyer values time.
 Buyer offers $17.8 M all-cash, 30-day close, if seller leaves $3 M in escrow refundable on environmental clean bill. Escrow releases to seller after Phase II passes or rolls into buyer Cap-Ex budget. Seller feels secure; buyer gets effective diligence window.

Deal closes; soil clean. Buyer's $200 k discount beats bridge interest; seller brags about fastest closing in county.

---

8 Case Study: Multifamily Rent-Control Buyout

Seventy-unit prewar building, half rent-controlled. Investor needs 20 units vacant to pencil total gut. Tenants organized; mediation tense.

Trade-Sheet Findings:
 Tenants fear relocation costs, school zones. Investor proposes staggered move-outs with bonuses:

- $25 k cash + moving van + first/last month new place

- Six-month transition for families so school year completes

- Option to return post-renovation at regulated formula

Sixty residents accept; litigation avoided; renovation starts two quarters earlier, saving $600 k carrying cost. Investor still profitable; tenants upgrade housing narrative.

---

9   Empathy Does Not Equal Weakness—Guardrails

Priam kneels but negotiates burial truce length to ensure proper rites. Compassion pairs with boundary.

Best Practices:

- Set BATNA privately.

- Grant concessions only against equal or higher reciprocal value.

- Deploy empathy early, firmness late.

- Put everything in writing within 24 hours.

- Use escrow and milestones to enforce.

---

10   When Empathy Fails—Countermeasures

Some Achilles never soften. If seller remains rigid:

- **Re-anchor with Data**—Market comps, cap-ex inspections.

- **Expand the Pie**—Bring mezz fund or JV partner to cover gap.

- **Change Time Horizon**—Offer master-lease; revisit price in three years.

- **Walk Away**—Signal strong BATNA; sometimes only distance resets stance.

Even Priam knew a single reckless word could forfeit Hector's corpse. Know your red line.

---

11   The Cultural Integration of Negotiation Mastery

- **War-Room Post-Mortems**—After each closing, list empathy moves that worked.

- **Shadowing Program**—Junior staff observe senior calls, note pivot moments.

- **Role-Play Drills**—One faction plays distressed seller, other plays urban-renewal fund. Switch roles; embody counterpart fears.

- **Deal Bible Updates**—Store successful concession bundles for quick reuse.

Compassion becomes muscle memory.

---

12   Final Reflection

"They remembered each man his own losses,
until dawn colored the sea, and the work of grieving
was done, and the work of returning could begin."

The king who humbled himself rescued more than a body; he extended Troy's life twelve sacred days, enough for rituals, farewells, and a last dignified moment. The investor who negotiates with open eyes and listening heart rescues more than margin; she preserves relationships, brand, and speed.

Treat every bargaining table like Achilles' fireside: a place where adversaries can become, if not friends, at least mutual guarantors of a shared story. Stack your trade-sheet, polish your empathy, and step into the tent ready to talk about fathers before you talk about price. The war will still be there outside—but inside, you may just find the ransom that buys peace, closes escrow, and leaves both parties stronger for having met.

Chapter 16 — The Funeral Games (Succession & Legacy)

Achilles has avenged Patroclus. Hector lies buried; Troy's fate is sealed. But the poem does not end in smoke and corpses. Instead, Homer lingers over funeral games—chariot races, boxing, discus, foot-races—held for a fallen friend. Weapons clang, prizes glitter, and heroes who were murdering each other yesterday now laugh, trade boasts, and hand down heirlooms to younger fighters. Why? Because every campaign, no matter how heroic, must transform from personal achievement into collective memory or it evaporates. The games are succession in motion: a structured ritual that converts victory into communal capital and trains replacements before dusk falls again.

> "So they honored the dead, and each man turned
> his mind to the gifts that tell of glory after life."

For ambitious real-estate investors, succession works the same magic. An empire of buildings, notes, and partnerships will eventually sift through probate unless it is moved—intentionally—into vessels that outlive the builder. Legacy is not a monument of granite; it is a living system that keeps distributing income, opportunity, and identity long after the first generation picks up the check. Funeral-game thinking is thus the last strategic discipline: celebrate the wins, codify the playbook, identify heirs, and embed the inheritance in structures that resist time, taxes, and family quarrel.

The Homeric Model of Legacy

Patroclus' games ring with three principles that translate directly into modern estate strategy.

1. Ritualized Wealth Transfer
Achilles lays out golden tripods, cauldrons, mules, horses, and forged swords. He then assigns each prize to a contest whose rules everyone knows. Disputes flare—Ajax fumes when a rival fumbles a throw—yet Achilles resolves them in public view. The games convert random booty into earned trophies, anchoring status not just on past deeds but on merit displayed today.

2. Public Recognition of Successors
New champions emerge. Antilochus, a younger noble, surprises grizzled racers by out-strategizing Menelaus on the track. Achilles applauds, and the army sees its next generation. By spotlighting fresh talent before the old guard dies, the army ensures continuity.

3. Closure Paired with Continuity
The contests finish, libations are poured, and dawn brings new action. The games give warriors space to release grief and reset ambition. Legacy is simultaneously a bridge and a drawbridge: it honors what ended and positions what continues.

Translating Funeral Games into Estate and Succession Planning

Stage One: The Inventory of Prizes

Before chariot wheels roll, list the estate's equivalent of tripods and horses:

- Real property (individual deeds, LLC membership interests, limited-partner units)

- Operating companies (development, construction, property management)

- Intellectual capital (underwriting models, vendor networks, proprietary data)

- Insurance policies and annuities

- Liquidity pools (cash, lines of credit, brokerage accounts)

- Digital assets (domain names, investor portals, deal rooms)

This inventory—ideally updated yearly—is step zero. Unknown assets cannot be placed in game brackets, and heirs cannot race for prizes they do not see.

Stage Two: Choosing the Arena

In the poem, Achilles matches skill to reward: charioteers vie for
the finest mare; boxers hammer each other for a sturdy cauldron.
Estate planners mimic that alignment by matching asset type to
legal wrapper:

- **Single-Asset Real-Estate LLC** → Transfer into a
  revocable living trust for probate avoidance and step-up
  in basis while retaining management flexibility.

- **Operating Companies** → Drop into a **family limited
  partnership (FLP)**; the founder holds general-partner
  voting control while gifting limited-partner equity over time
  to children at minority and lack-of-marketability discounts.

- **Long-Term Hold Portfolios** → Shelter in **dynasty trusts**
  (APT or GST-exempt) that postpone estate tax for multiple
  generations.

- **Liquid Cash Reserves** → Pack into **irrevocable
  life-insurance trusts (ILITs)** or **spousal lifetime-access
  trusts (SLATs)** to remove future appreciation from taxable
  estate while keeping emergency draw flexibility.

- **Philanthropic Assets** → Assign to **donor-advised funds**
  or **private foundations**, turning capital-gain avoidance into
  brand equity and tax deduction.

Match each subclass the way Achilles matches competitors to
events.

Stage Three: Drafting the Playbook

Games run smoothly because everyone understands the rules. A modern investor's rulebook includes:

- **Operating Agreements** that specify dead-man clauses, key-man insurance beneficiaries, step-in authority for successor managers, and buy-sell pricing formulas.

- **Investment Policy Statement (IPS)** summarizing target geographies, risk tolerance, leverage caps, and ethical guardrails.

- **Capital Call Protocols** designating who has the right—but not the obligation—to fund new deals once the founder is gone.

- **Distribution Policies** clarifying waterfall order, reinvestment thresholds, and liquidity targets.

Write them, notarize them, store them in both hard copy and encrypted cloud. Include a plain-language cheat sheet: even Homer repeats catalogues so warriors memorize lineage.

Stage Four: Choosing and Training Heirs

Achilles does not toss reins to anyone who wanders by; he hands the first prize to Diomedes because battle experience proves worth. Real-estate dynasts must identify successors by competence, not birth order alone:

1. Create a **skills matrix** spanning acquisition analysis, capital markets, construction oversight, and investor relations.

2. Score each candidate—child, niece, long-time COO, or outside protégé—on mastery and passion.

3. Build rotational programs: six months in financing, six in operations, six in asset management.

4. Pair each rotation with *decision rights*, not just observation. Let them sign contracts within limits; debrief successes and missteps.

5. Formalize mentorship: weekly one-on-ones documenting lessons.

Titles follow competence. In athletic contests, the laurel means the runner beat the field; in family business, the leadership seat must prove likewise.

Stage Five: Communication and Celebration

The army watches Achilles award prizes with loud proclamations; everyone sees fairness and finality. Similarly, heirs and investors need ceremonial transparency:

- **Family Retreats** where founders present the estate plan, explain rationale, encourage questions.

- **Investor Summits** announcing successor leadership long before transition.

- **Public Milestones**—naming scholarships, sponsoring park renovations—signal brand continuity.

Ceremony transforms legal paper into social fact. When the founder finally passes, confusion cannot ignite because the games were already played in daylight.

The Mechanics of Estate Vehicles

The Revocable Living Trust (RLT)

Like Achilles' palm over the chariot reins, the founder retains absolute authority while alive. Assets avoid probate courts, remain private, and receive step-up in basis at death—erasing latent capital gains. Upon incapacity, successor trustees slide into control within hours, maintaining lender continuity clauses and property-management contracts.

The Family Limited Partnership (FLP)

General-partner units (often 1–2 %) carry voting power; the balance sits in non-voting limited interests. Gifting schedules exploit valuation discounts, reducing gift-tax impact. If a limited partner faces divorce or creditor claims, charging-order protections prevent forced sale.

Dynasty or GST-Exempt Trusts

Structured to outlive estate-tax resets, these trusts cap distributions at unitized percentages of trust net value, preserving principal. Trustees may invest in future deals, ensuring compounding continues. Some states allow perpetual trusts; others cap at 360 years. Choose domicile (South Dakota, Delaware, Nevada) carefully.

Directed Trusts

Split duties: an **investment committee** oversees asset allocation; a **distribution committee** approves beneficiary requests; an **administrative trustee** handles filings. This mirrors Achilles delegating boxing oversight to Epeius and chariot judging to Antilochus—checks and balances curb rashness.

Cross-Generational Mentoring Programs

Just as funeral games test and teach younger heroes, a succession-oriented enterprise embeds three pipelines.

Shadow Boards
 A junior council analyzes one deal per quarter and presents to senior board. Feedback loops produce confidence and reveal talent.

Joint-Venture Laboratories
 Give protégés a small equity slug in lower-risk deals; let them

negotiate debt, manage Cap-Ex, file quarterly reports. Failure cost is tuition; success proves stewardship.

Legacy Case Studies
Once a month, dissect historical wins and losses—"Remember the 2015 student-housing fiasco"—extract lessons, and codify into the IPS.

Failure Modes and Iliadic Warnings

Homer's epilogue mentions only briefly the destiny of Achilles' captured loot; many spoils vanish as Greeks bicker during the voyage home. Estate plans fail for similar reasons:

- **Undefined Governance**—No trustee succession triggers court appointment; heirs sue.

- **Undivided Control Assets**—Ten siblings inherit 100 % of a single hotel; stalemate halts renovations.

- **Liquidity Mismatch**—Death taxes or buy-sell obligations force fire sale at market trough.

- **Silent Equities**—Founder hoards knowledge; when he dies, lenders call loans on bewildered heirs.

- **Ego Contest**—Heirs replay chariot race scandals, dragging legacy into court.

Mitigate each by leaning on the Funeral Game model: public scoring, matched prizes, transparent rulings.

Action Steps: The Legacy Blueprint Worksheet

1. **Life-Mission Headline**
   In one sentence, state what the empire should achieve beyond your lifetime.

2. **Asset Ledger**
   List every property, entity, lien, partner, insurance, and digital credential.

3. **Vehicle Map**
   Draw arrows from each asset to trust, FLP, ILIT, or foundation. Include successor names.

4. **Heir Skills Matrix**
   Columns: Acquisition, Finance, Construction, Ops, Investor Relations. Rows: Candidates. Fill ratings 1–5.

5. **Mentorship Calendar**
   Outline rotations, coaches, evaluation checkpoints for the next three years.

6. **Liquidity Stress-Test**
   Model estate-tax liability, buy-sell triggers, key-man debt

covenants. Identify sources: life insurance, cash, lines.

7. **Communication Plan**
   Draft presentation decks: Family Retreat, Investor
   Webinar, Lender Memo.

8. **Philanthropy Sheet**
   Causes, dollar targets, governance rules for
   donor-advised fund or foundation.

9. **Timeline Gantt**
   Assign completion dates: legal docs six months, funding
   trusts nine months, first shadow board meeting twelve
   months.

10. **Annual Review Trigger**
    Set recurrence in project-management software; review
    trust performance, heir progress, IPS relevance.

Complete the worksheet, notarize key pages, and distribute
encrypted copies to attorney, CPA, and lead heir. Store originals in
fireproof safe. Update after every major acquisition or family
milestone.

Closing Reflection: Torchlight for the Long Night

Funeral games are raucous—blood, sweat, broken axle
spokes—yet their purpose is quiet resilience. Achilles will die on

the Scamander plain; Odysseus will wander ten more years; Ajax will fall on his sword. But the memory and methods encoded in the games travel forward: chariot wheels echo in Roman circus, discus arcs in Olympic stadiums, and the gold tripods melted perhaps into coins that funded colonies abroad. Legacy outlives architects when structure harnesses story.

> "So the sons of the Achaeans went their ways,
> bearing the prizes, proud of the deeds done,
> and the tale of long spears followed them
> into lands unborn."

Design your estate to do likewise. Let every LLC agreement, trust clause, apprenticeship rotation, and philanthropy grant serve as one more polished discus sailing into the dusk—a continuous arc binding your name to the hopes of heirs who will never meet you but will thank you with the quiet certainty of opportunity inherited, games prepared, and torches kept alight.

The war is won, the fires banked, the field cleared. Now the legacy begins.

Conclusion – The Endless Epic

The hulls have launched, the torches have guttered out, and Homer's bronze-clad combatants are memories on the wind—but real estate markets keep seething like the wine-dark sea. Every cycle sprinkles fresh Troys along rivers, highways, and commuter rails; every decade summons new Agamemnons, Hectors, and Achilleses into bidding rooms and loan committees. If you have marched through all sixteen chapters of this playbook, you now carry a war chest of frameworks that turn myth into underwriting, quarrel into deal structure, and rage into disciplined asset strategy.

Yet the epic is "endless" because mastery never closes. The moment you finish a victorious exit, the sands beneath your next acquisition are already shifting—rates twitch, councils vote, tenants migrate. Homer's enduring message is that heroes do not win once; they **continue winning by practicing habits that outlast any single triumph**. What follows is a synthesis of those habits, drawn from the lessons you've traced across siege walls, funeral games, and midnight truces. Engrave them on your underwriting binder, tack them above your modeling monitor, or weave them into the partnership charter that guides your firm.

HABITS FOR LIFELONG CAMPAIGNERS

1. **Name the Prize Before You Lift the Shield.**
   Just as the Greeks fought "till Ilios falls," every acquisition, rehab, refi, or sale needs a line-item objective with a date.

If you cannot state the goal in one breath, you lack a goal.

2. **Gather Coalitions, Not Crowds.**
   Agamemnon's greatest triumph was welding fifty quarrelsome kings into a single spearhead. Curate lenders, contractors, attorneys, and equity partners who share your thesis; prune the rest.

3. **Model Emotion, Then Delete It.**
   Achilles' wrath nearly sunk the fleet. Run pre-offer stress tests, decision logs, and blind-comp underwriting so that ego and fear appear on paper—then strip them from the final model.

4. **Sharpen Risk Armor Relentlessly.**
   Hephaestus gave Achilles a multidimensional shield. Re-shop insurance, refresh rate caps, audit entities, and test incident drills every quarter. An asset dies the day the owner stops polishing bronze.

5. **Outthink When You Can't Outmuscle.**
   If conventional leverage fails, build a Trojan Horse: seller notes, lease-options, equity swaps. Creativity beats size nine times in ten.

6. **Maintain the Wall Every Dawn.**
   Hector checked stones even when the city toasted. Tenant retention touchpoints, weekly maintenance walk-throughs, and twelve-month ops calendars are the mortar between distributions.

7. **Scan the Sky for Divine Whims.**
   Zoning boards, tax writers, and central banks are gods in
   modern armor. Install macro-risk dashboards and scenario
   drills; adjust sails before thunder cracks.

8. **Time Surges Like Achilles.**
   Capital injections and re-brands work only when they slam
   the market at peak complacency. Track competing supply,
   rate windows, and demographic pulses; strike once and
   hard.

9. **Retreat Faster Than You Fell in Love.**
   Hector fell because he lingered outside the gate. Use
   hold/sell decision trees and 1031 ladders; exit an
   underperformer as soon as metrics cross your red line.

10. **Exit With Ceremony, Not Haste.**
   Victory is pronounced when cash wires clear. Write exit
   maps on day one—waterfalls, tax shields, broker RFP
   timelines—and rehearse them annually.

11. **Negotiate Through Shared Humanity.**
   Priam's ransom shows that empathy unsticks deadlocks.
   Learn counterpart fears, draft concession trade-sheets,
   and let joint wins enlarge the pie.

12. **Teach the Games Before the Funeral.**
   Legacy begins while founders breathe. Rotate heirs
   through decision seats, fund dynasty trusts, document
   playbooks, and celebrate small successes in public.

13. **Keep Writing the Poem.**
Homer ends on a funeral feast, implying life continues.
Reflect after each deal: lessons, mile-stones, errors.
Archive post-mortems so new associates start one stanza
further along.

THE ILIAD INVESTOR CODE   (One-Page Quick Reference)

1. OATH OF PURPOSE
— State your buy-box and exit horizon in <20 words.
— Reject every deal that misses one criterion.

2. COALITION RULE
— Three calls to vet every ally (track record, communication rhythm, fee clarity).
— Written charter, signed before LOI.

3. RAGE FILTER
— Pre-offer stress test: identify ego, fear, FOMO; recalibrate numbers.
— Maintain decision log with 50-word rationale for each major choice.

4. SHIELD PROTOCOL
— Quarterly gap-analysis worksheet on insurance, entities, hedges, and processes.
— Emergency liquidity $\geq$ 6 months fixed expenses.

5. TROJAN TOOLKIT

— Creative financing menu: seller carry, lease-option, equity swap, pref equity.

— Deals must pencil under both conventional and creative funding.

6. WALL MAINTENANCE CYCLE

— 12-month ops calendar; weekly exterior walk; monthly KPI dashboard.

— Renewal calls 90 days before lease-end.

7. GODS' WATCHLIST

— Macro-risk radar: zoning agendas, tax bills, Fed signals.
— Stress test NOI at +500 bps interest and −20 % rent.

8. SURGE WINDOW

— Reposition only when NOI plateau + supply pause + cheap capital intersect.

— Feasibility grid: physical, financial, market, operational, exit.

9. RETREAT CLAUSE

— Hold/Sell tree reviewed every year.
— Trigger exit when two negative signals persist two quarters.

10. EXIT MANUAL

— Exit-mapping template ready at acquisition.
— Broker whisper 6 months out; appraisal file current; data room pre-loaded.

11. RANSOM ETHIC

— Open with empathy; trade low-cost/high-value concessions.
— Everything in writing within 24 hours.

12. LEGACY LOOP
  — Annual asset ledger + trust funding check.
  — Shadow board for next gen; family retreat disclosure.

A Last Word to the Campaigner

You will reread market reports that contradict each other. You will stand in half-demoed hallways wondering if the Fed will hike tomorrow. You will negotiate clauses at 2 a.m. with sellers who swear "take it or leave it," only to concede after coffee. Some months you will stare at red-ink dashboards and feel the Greek darkness creeping toward your ships.

That is when you recall Homer's long arc: the heroes win not because they are flawless but because they persist through every reversal armed with craft, courage, and comradeship. The *Iliad* never promised a painless road; it promised that glory belongs to those who keep marching, adapt their tactics, care for their team, and never forget the human stakes behind every stone wall and every line of pro-forma.

Carry this code, practice the habits, and keep your own epic alive. When you one day host funeral games—whether for a project, a partnership, or a founder—you'll know the contests were fair, the prizes meaningful, and the legacy secure. Then, like Homer's warriors launching homeward across a blazing horizon, you can face the next venture with calm eyes and seasoned steel, ready to write the next canto on the restless sea of deals that awaits beyond the breaker line.

THIS IS NOT A COLLECTION

This volume is part of **Ancient Wisdom Hacks**—
an ongoing body of work focused on how strategy, power, and
failure actually function under pressure.

The books are only one layer.

What you are reading is an entry point into a larger system of
interpretation, application, and expansion.

WHAT THESE WORKS ARE DESIGNED TO DO

Most people look for answers.

These works expose patterns:

- How decisions are made before they are visible
- How systems weaken before they collapse
- How power shifts before it is recognized

This is not theory.
It is applied observation.

THE SYSTEM BEHIND THE WORK

Across all volumes and future releases, three forces remain
constant:

- **Strategy** — how outcomes are shaped before action
- **Conflict** — how people and systems break under pressure
- **Power** — how control is gained, maintained, and lost

No single book contains the full picture.
Each adds another angle.

CONTINUE BEYOND THIS VOLUME

New interpretations, applied volumes, and extended works are released continuously.

To access current and future material, visit:

www.AncientWisdomHacks.com

WHAT YOU WILL FIND

- Additional applied volumes across industries
- Expanded interpretations of foundational texts
- New releases not available through standard distribution
- Future projects extending beyond books

The system is still expanding.

FINAL POSITION

Clarity does not make outcomes easier.

It removes the illusion that they were ever simple.

Ancient Wisdom Hacks
Interpretation over repetition.
Application over theory.